A Book of Cookery

A
Book of Cookery for
dressing of severall
dishes of Meate and
makeing of severall
sauces and seasoning
for meat or Foule

A Book of Cookery

for dressing of Several Dishes of Meat and making of Several Sauces and Seasoning for Meat or Fowl

By
Hannah Alexander

Edited by
Deirdre Nuttall

With an Introduction by
Jennifer Nuttall *née* Alexander

evertype
2014

Published by Evertype, Cnoc Sceichín, Leac an Anfa, Cathair na Mart, Co. Mhaigh Eo, Éire. www.evertype.com.

A catalogue record for this book is available from the British Library.

ISBN-10 1-78201-074-2
ISBN-13 978-1-78201-074-6

Set in Caslon, 1741 *Financière Italic*, and *1741* **FINANCIERE TITL ITALIC** by Michael Everson.

Cover design by Michael Everson. Photographs by Michael Everson. Frontispiece photograph by Edward Delaney.

Printed by LightningSource.

Table of Contents

Note: Recipes in the table of contents below were written by Hannah the Elder, unless followed by (HD) standing for Hannah Dorothea, or by (HF) for "Hannah's Friend" indicating one of the other hands which appear to have added a recipe here and there to the book over the years. Culinary or other recipes which were originally found in the "Medicines and cures" section but have been moved are indicated by the Staff of Aesculapius: ⚕.

Part I

A BOOK OF COOKERY

Introduction

A recipe book from the 1680s is a rare find—but we found it, opened it, and discovered that we could read it with ease and look up the recipes in the hand-made index—*How to Candy Ringo Roots*, and *Vennyson: To keep a Year*, and *Aqua Mirabilis*, and many, many more.

This *Book of Cookery*, written by Hannah Alexander with additional recipes by her daughter, Hannah Dorothea, is the result of our find and of years of work, both by the authors and by their descendants. You will read some extraordinary recipes, some that you will want to try out immediately, some that are very strange, and some that are definitely just to read! (Do try the *Orange Fool*; it is easy and delicious and features regularly on our dinner tables.)

Although the recipe book is unique, it is also typical of its time. Similar recipes are mentioned in Mary Ogle's book from Wexford,[1] in Mary Delany's Letters[2] and those recorded in *Mary Cannon's Commonplace Book* which survives in transcript form, although the original has been lost.[3] Hannah's English shows a number of loanwords from Gaelic, either

1   Ogle, 1713.
2   Delaney, 1991.
3   Quarton, 2010.

Scottish or Irish, notably, the use of "slew" (from *slua*) to mean "a lot".

Spelling was not standardized when Mrs Hannah Alexander, the primary author, and her daughter Hannah Dorothea Madden were writing. Nouns were frequently given a capital letter. There are some recipes in which the same word is written in various different ways even in the context of a single page. The word *manchet* from French, meaning "a loaf of white bread", is written as *manshot* and *manshott*, for example. Words are written phonetically, which can pose a challenge to the modern reader. In one example we were puzzled by the title *to pickle herons*, only to find from the context that the author was referring to *herrings*.

While Hannah Alexander went to great effort to write the book neatly and even included an index, we don't know the provenance of most of the recipes, although a few of the later ones are attributed to women who must have been friends of Hannah Dorothea. Presumably many were transcribed from published sources, from others' handwritten "Commonplace Books" and so forth. Whatever the case, the recipes provide a fascinating insight into how middle class Irish people ate at the time.

About the authors

Documents relating to our family give quite a bit of information about the Alexander men, but almost nothing about the women, so what we know about Hannah and Hannah Dorothea is largely pieced together from our knowledge of the men in their lives.

Hannah Browne, of Irish or Scottish descent, married James Alexander in 1685, and she and her husband lived in Great Ship Street, Dublin, close to Dublin Castle where James was employed. Hannah was James's second wife; his first wife, a daughter of Peter Blanchville, was from Kilkenny and had borne three children by James. James, who was originally from Paisley (now part of greater Glasgow), was employed at the time of his marriage to Hannah Browne as Clerk in the Exchequer Court of Dublin Castle dealing with Revenue accounts, known nowadays as Income Tax. Hannah and James attended the Anglican Church of St James in Dublin.

According to family records, Hannah Dorothea was born "upon the Lord's Day 24th of October 1686, exactly at three in the afternoon and was baptized the ninth day of November 1686 at Dublin by Dean William Lloyd." Hannah Dorothea had twin brothers, Richard and John, who were born in Paisley, Scotland in 1690, where the family had gone to escape the civil unrest in Ireland that culminated in the Battle of the Boyne. Afterwards, the family returned to live in Dublin, and James died in 1701. The family clearly cherished their Scottish links, as the head of each generation of the Alexander family continued to apply to be a Baillie (or councillor) of the City of Glasgow until the end of the nineteenth century.

When Hannah Dorothea grew up she married a man called John McLellan. After his death she married Thomas Madden, a medical doctor, who lectured in the School of Anatomy in Trinity College. They lived in Aungier Street in Dublin, around the corner from her childhood home and just five minutes' walk from Trinity College. Sadly, Hannah Dorothea had no children, and perhaps this is why so little is known of the two Hannahs, as there was no one to pass on family history and the lives of women were rarely recorded in much detail.

In 1734 Thomas Madden died "of a fever" and Hannah Dorothea moved to New Ross in Co. Wexford to live with her unmarried nephew, Arthur Price Alexander, in his home on Priory Street. She probably moved because life was less expensive in a small town and, as a widow, it would have been easier to maintain her standard of living. New Ross, a river port market town in inland Wexford, situated along the banks of the wide river Barrow, was a pleasant place to live in and Hannah was surrounded by her relatives. She brought her recipe book with her, so she must have had the expectation of being able to continue eating (and drinking) well, despite her reduced circumstances.

Hannah Dorothea's brother, John Alexander, a leather and coal merchant in the town, lived on the Quay in New Ross, and he was also briefly connected with salt panning in Slade on Wexford's Hook Peninsula (the ruins of the salt houses are still visible on the quay in Slade). John died in 1767, and in his will he left "five pounds to my dear sister Madden to buy mourning clothes." We have portraits of James and John Alexander, and of Arthur Price. They look like kind people, but it's a shame not to be able to see what either of the Hannahs looked like.

For someone who evidently had inherited her mother's love of food, New Ross was a good choice. As it was an active port town, ships regularly delivered the spices and exotic ingredients that both Hannahs used in their cooking. The rich cuisine of New Ross was mentioned in 1684, shortly before Hannah Dorothea was born. In *An Account of ye towne of New Rosse in ye countye of Wexforde, and of some of the Baronies there, this 29th March 1684*, Robert Leigh of Rosegarland, an estate-owner from south Wexford, writes that although the town had been badly damaged during the 1641 Rebellion, it had "pretty good trading for wine and fruits out of Spaine and France, and alsoe for transporting of beefe, hydes and tallow.[4] Leigh also mentions that the countryside around Ross was noted for hunting and hawking. There was plenty of game, especially pheasant, grouse and hare.

Whereas Hannah Alexander, and Hannah Dorothea during her marriages, had lived in Dublin where there was a large and very secure Protestant population, Hannah Dorothea had moved into a very different environment. Although the small Protestant population in the area throughout the eighteenth century was increasingly prosperous, they were very aware of being a resented minority and they were anxious about it. In 1730, the New Ross Corporation sent a petition to Dublin Castle, requesting the reversal of a

4   Hore, 2007, 201.

decision to remove some of the troops in the area. Without them the petitioners felt "utterly defenceless and exposed to the fury and outrage of a disaffected riotous populace."[5] The petition was signed by the sovereign, burgesses, freemen and other Protestant inhabitants of the town, including Hannah Dorothea's brother, John Alexander. The petition was written following three years of poor harvests caused by bad weather. Prices were high and a lot of food crops were lost—including potatoes, which were already an essential source of food for the poor, and widely eaten by other social classes too.

Ireland's food culture in historical context

The Alexanders were lucky to have enough money to cook and enjoy rich food at a time when many went hungry. Given the amount of butter, sugar and alcohol in the recipes in the book, one hopes that they didn't eat like this every day. A well-known contemporary of Hannah's (albeit from a much more aristocratic family), Mary Delany, wrote in one of her many letters to her niece in England regarding her husband's eating habits "the greatest feast to him is a fried egg and bacon."[6] That's one Irish taste that hasn't changed!

A diary entry written by Dorothea Herbert describing her life and times in 1767 in the parish of Knock

5   Ibid, 206-7.
6   Day, 1991, 170.

Grafton, Carrick on Suir, where her father was the Rector, offers vibrant descriptions of how well the family ate: "We sit down morning, noon, and night to the finest beef in Christendom, (for we always bought a quarter whenever Mr Roe killed one of his remarkable cows)—we had besides every kind of fruit and vegetable from Rockwell—The finest young sucking pigs from Mrs Dexter—The finest fat geese from Mrs Dogherty, with quantities of eggs, butter, cream cheeses, and oaten cakes all gratis, except the 200 pound weight of beef which we paid for... besides other good things we had remarkable chocolate, as Cashel was famous for it."[7]

Allowing for some exaggeration in Dorothea Herbert's account (she was always anxious to give a good impression) her diary shows that, if they had the resources, rural people could eat as well as city folk. Like Dorothea Herbert, Hannah Dorothea probably received gifts of game, fruit and vegetables from friends and acquaintances in the area.

Account books from the large estates in Ireland at the time note that they often produced surplus fruits and vegetables that were sold off from the hothouses and walled gardens, enabling the purchase of such exotica as pineapple, peaches and apricots.[8] Local newspapers of the time also show an interest among local gardeners in producing a range of vegetables.[9]

A 1776 advertisement in the *Waterford Chronicle* newspaper for John Winckworth's grocery business in

7   Herbert, 2004, 197.
8   Barnard, 2005, 27-35.
9   Barnard, 2004, 219.

the main street of New Ross shows that a wide selection of goods was available. In both Dublin and New Ross Hannah and Hannah Dorothea were able to find the exotic ingredients that many of their recipes call for. Ingredients which seem exotic to us today may have been much less so several centuries ago. Happily for Hannah Dorothea, John Winckworth was connected to the family by marriage—no doubt he could help her when she wanted to prepare a special meal by ordering what she needed, and perhaps offering a discount!

Most of the recipes in this book seem extraordinarily lavish to a modern reader. Rice pudding, for example, requires two quarts of cream, twelve eggs, suet, a pound of sugar, and ambergris, nutmeg and mace. A similar recipe is recorded in *The English Housewife*, written by Gervase Markham in 1615. Gervase describes the ingredients being mixed together, then stuffed into cleaned pig or sheep intestines, first boiled and then placed on a gridiron over a fire.[10] Boiled puddings like this, or like plum pudding, were served together with the meat; some were cooked directly underneath the roasting beef to soak up the juices of the meat. The now quintessential Scottish dish, haggis, as described in this book and in others, is similarly made.[11]

This book, as well as others written at the time, refers to the heavy use of spices, and to the great variety of spices and flavourings available then. Spiced foods had been fashionable throughout

10   Markham, 2011.
11   Ogle, 1713.

Europe since the late Middle Ages, having been introduced by crusaders and pilgrims returning from their rampages in "the Holy Land". British priories record having fennel, ginger, saffron, garlic, pepper, and cloves in the fourteenth century. At that time the difficulties in obtaining spices, and the romance and mystique that surrounded the spice trade, ensured that they remained extremely expensive and accessible only to the very wealthy in England and Ireland.[12]

Throughout the sixteenth century the trade in pepper, cloves, nutmeg and mace was monopolised almost completely by the Portuguese. The Dutch controlled the Spice Islands (the Molucca Islands and Banda Islands in Malaysia) until well into the seventeenth century. By the end of the sixteenth century spices were cheaper and more widely available, largely because saplings of spice trees had been transplanted in other tropical areas. Nations with colonial and trading ambitions, like the British and French, entered the market. Competition and greater availability forced down the market price. In consequence spices became much more widely available, even to people with relatively modest incomes. As well as enjoying the spices for their exotic flavours, people believed that spices helped to preserve meat as well as flavour it (the strong spicy flavours would disguise the taste of putrid meat, although they are not actually very good at preserving it). Salt and saltpetre, which are mentioned in this book, were used to preserve food.

12   Norman, 1990, 12.

Meat and fish were spiced with cinnamon, pepper, cloves, nutmeg, ginger and saffron, as well as more familiar garden herbs like thyme and marjoram. Capsicums, allspice and vanilla had already been introduced as medicines from the Americas in the sixteenth century and were now used in cooking. Queen Elizabeth's (1533-1603) apothecary recommended using vanilla as a flavouring rather than a drug (our recipe book does not mention vanilla, however). One of the medicinal recipes below uses "mirch" or what is now known as capsicum or chilli peppers, a native plant of Central America. The word "mirch" comes from Hindi and is the name for pepper, and "lal" is the name for chilli, showing that the trade had gone in a circuitous fashion from the Americas to India (introduced there by the Portuguese) and from India to England.[13]

The British East India Company was founded in 1600 in an effort to wrest the lucrative spice trade away from the Dutch East India Company. Until then the English had a minor role in the trade. By 1700 the company was trading chiefly in indigo, saltpetre, long peppers and tea, as well as chocolate and coffee beans. That great diarist of London life in the mid seventeenth century, Samuel Pepys, wrote excitedly on 16th November 1665 about a vessel of the Dutch East Indies fleet captured by the English. The whole vessel was stuffed with pepper, cloves and nutmeg and he waded through the spices, which came up to his knees. A year later, during the Great Fire of London, he buried Parmesan cheese and wine in his

---

13   Keay, 2006, 250.

garden to save it from being looted or burnt. At this time there was increased receptivity to new things— new ideas, new religions, new political systems, and new food. Pepys's diaries emphasise the gradual change in eating habits amongst the English, fuelled by the increasing trade with continental Europe.

In the turbulent years of Oliver Cromwell's Commonwealth many wealthy Royalist supporters of Charles II were forced into exile in France, following Henrietta Maria, the French wife of King Charles the First, who had been executed. There, they were welcomed by the French King. During their exile they became accustomed to the much more varied diet in France and, following the restoration of Charles II to the throne, must have brought their preferences back to England and on to Ireland.

During the Commonwealth, many French chefs living in England had published recipe books to make a living because their extravagant cooking was not popular during this puritanical time. French terms such as "fricassee" and "ragout" gradually became familiar from the new recipe books, along with ingredients such as capers, anchovies (the Hannahs were great lovers of anchovies) and of course the coffee and chocolate that Pepys refers to so often.

In the seventeenth and eighteenth centuries anyone who could afford to ate a huge amount of meat. In fact, the word "meat" was often used as a collective noun when referring to food in general. When the Hannahs were writing their book, the middle and upper classes of Ireland seem to have eaten ever greater amounts of meat, as did the

English (because of the closer contact between Ireland and England and the settlement of English people in different parts of the country). At the same time, the poor ate ever more potatoes until, by the early nineteenth century, they were almost completely dependent on them.

The change in Ireland's diet is reflective of the great cultural changes that were underway. As well as the colonisers and planters from Scotland and England (including the Alexanders), Huguenots and other groups from Western Europe were encouraged to settle in Ireland from the 1660s onwards. As they gradually established themselves in different areas in Ireland, their influence on dietary habits would have been felt. The Palatines arrived in the eighteenth century, again bringing their own distinct culture and tradition, along with their eating habits. At the aristocratic end of the social spectrum, many young men such as Lord Edward Fitzgerald, favourite son of Emily, Duchess of Leinster, went on the Grand Tour of Europe, learned to enjoy foreign food, and would have wanted it on their return.

Foreign tastes and methods of cookery steadily permeated the cities and larger towns of Ireland and England, but not everyone was enamoured of the new trends in cooking. In her book *The Art of Cookery Made Plain and Easy* Hannah Glasse writes disparagingly of French customs, saying, "So much is the blind folly of this age, that they would rather be imposed on by a French booby, than give encouragement to a good English cook.[14]

In Ireland, Dorothea Herbert refers to an "old French Woman (who) came begging to us". The lady stayed with the family, teaching them French and introducing them to such dishes as *soupe maigre*, and salad greens. Dorothea also refers to a French cook who served their dinner under the trees; another example of how new ideas were spread.[15]

For centuries, Ireland's extensive coastline had facilitated the legal and illegal importation of French and Spanish wines. For those who could afford them, foodstuffs were imported too. In 1753, when Hannah Dorothea was still using this book, the Dublin Directory of that year shows that there was a demand for all these goods. Smaller ports like New Ross benefited from increased trade as roads and travel improved. According to the Directory, trade from Portugal that year included, "Wine, salt, fruits, oranges, lemons, oil of almonds, figs, saffron, soap, white marble, liquorice, sumac, [a small tree grown now for autumn colour]", from France, "Tobacco, wine, brandy, fine lace, Geneva, vinegar, hoops, [hops?], cork, liquorice, syrup of capillaire [maidenhair fern], Hungary water [rosemary juice] perfumes, rosin, jessamine [jasmine] oil, walnut oil, sweetmeats, sugar moulds, verdigris, capers, olives, prunes, anchovies, almonds, salad oil, turpentine," and from the sugar plantations in the Virgin Islands, Antigua, Montserrat, and Barbuda, (an island in the eastern Caribbean) "Anguilla, pyn [pineapple?], tamarins [tamarind], lime juice."[16]

---

14   Glasse, 2011, 4.
15   Herbert, 2004, 83.

An Irish Kitchen

In the seventeenth and early eighteenth centuries cooking was done over an open fire using gridirons and spits and in the pot oven. Kettles were boiled hanging from a crane (still familiar in Ireland in the 1950s). Ranges were developed in the eighteenth century with an open fire in the middle with a boiler for water and/or an oven on either side. The bread oven built beside the hearth in our home dates from around 1750 when the farmhouse was built, and is probably typical of bread ovens in medium-sized homes in both town and countryside; the Hannahs probably had similar ovens at their disposal. Large joints of meat were cooked on rotating jacks turned by hand or by smoke from the fire, and pots and pans were either copper or cast iron. Smoked ham and bacon hung from iron hooks in the kitchen ceiling, and flour and oatmeal were kept in barrels near the hearth to keep them dry.[17] A nearby pantry or larder in which to store food must have been an enticing place for aspiring cooks and children, judging by the frequent references in contemporary literature such as *The Vicar of Wakefield* by Oliver Goldsmith or *History of the Fairchild Family* by Mary Sherwood.

---

16   Dublin Directory, 1753, 40-3.
17   http://www.esb.ie/main/about-esb/numbertwentynine/
     virtual_tour/basement.htm (16 November 2011).

INTRODUCTION

The Hannahs' legacy

Hannah's *A Book of Cookery* is so well presented, with a clear and correct index, and precise directions as to how dishes are to be prepared, that we wonder if she had planned to publish it, and maybe passed the task of finding a publisher on to Hannah Dorothea. But Hannah Dorothea didn't publish it, and because she had no children we know very little about her—there was nobody to pass on stories of her likes and dislikes, hopes and dreams. We do know that her relatives must have esteemed and respected her as the family records contain three separate notes about her birth, marriages and death. Letitia Alexander, a descendant of Hannah's, living in the nineteenth century, added her name to the inside cover of *A Book of Cookery*, so presumably she was the person who saved Hannah's book when the house on Priory St was rented out after the last family member to live there died. We can only imagine most of the details of the lives of the women—Hannah Alexander and Hannah Dorothea—who wrote this book and left it for us to find.

Hannah Dorothea died aged 87 in 1773, nearly a hundred years after her mother began writing this book, and she is buried in St Mary's Churchyard, in New Ross. Given her great age, a lifetime of wining and dining had clearly done her no harm whatsoever. Let that be an example to us all.

Jennifer Nuttall *née* Alexander

Bibliography and further reading

Alexander, Arthur Vickers. [c. 1930]. *History of the Alexander family in Ireland and Scotland, from 1660*. (Unpublished manuscript.)

Allen, David E. & Hatfield, Gabrielle. 2004. *Medicinal Plants in Folk Tradition: An Ethnobotany of Britain & Ireland*. Portland & Cambridge: Timber Press. 0-88192-638-8

Anonymous. 1908. *A Book of Simples*. London: Sampson Low, Marston and Co. (Originally eighteenth century.)

Bardwell, Frances. 1930. *The Herb Garden*. London: A & C Black.

Barnard, Toby. 2005. *A Guide to Sources for the History of Material Culture in Ireland, 1500–2000*. Dublin & Portland: Four Courts Press. 1851829512

Barnard, Toby. 2004. *Making the Grand Figure: Lives and Possessions in Ireland, 1641-1770*. New Haven & London: Yale University Press. 0300204264

Creighton, Helen. 1950. *Folklore from Lunenburg County, Nova Scotia*. National Museum of Canada, Bulletin No. 117, Anthropological Series No. 29.

Clarkson, Leslie and Margaret Crawford. 2002. *Feast and Famine: Food and Nutrition in Ireland 1500–1920*. Oxford: Oxford University Press. 0198227515

Hughes, Anne. 1981. *The Diary of a Farmer's Wife 1796–1797*. Edited by Jeanne Preston. London: Penguin. 0140157069

Culpeper, Nicholas. [s.d.]. *Culpepper's British Herbal*. London: Foulsham and Co.

Day, Angelique (ed.). 1991. *Letters from Georgian Ireland: the correspondence of Mary Delany, 1731-68*. Belfast: Friar's Bush Press. 094687235X

Dublin Directory for the year 1753.

Dunne, Tom (ed.). 2007. *New Ross, Rosponte, Ros Mhic Treoin. An Anthology Celebrating 800 Years*. Ardcavan: Wexford County Council Public Library Service. 9780955146763

Glasse, Hannah. 2012. (1747.) *The Art of Cookery Made Plain and Easy, in Everlasting Syllabub and the Art of Carving*. Blackawton, Totnes: Prospect Books. 1903018889

Grigson, Geoffry. 1955. *The Englishman's Flora*. London: Phoenix House.

Herbert, Dorothea. 2004. *Retrospections of Dorothea Herbert, 1770–1806*. Dublin: Townhouse.

Hore, H. F. 2007. "Ross at the end of the seventeenth century", in Tom Dunne (ed.) *New Ross, Rosponte, Ros Mhic Treoin. An Anthology celebrating 800 years*. Ardcavan: Wexford County Council Public Library Service. 9780955146763

Keay, John. 2006. *The Spice Route: A History*. London: John Murray. 071956199X

Kidder, Edward. [c.1720]. *Receipts of Pastry and Cookery for the use of his Scholars*. London: [s.n.].

Markham, Gervase. 1615. *The English Housewife, London*. [http://wwwhistoricfood.com/English. Retrieved 12 November 2013.]

Norman, Jill. 1990. *The Complete Book of Spices*. London: Dorling Kindersley. 0863184871

Ogle, Mary. 1713. *A Book of Receiths*. Ms. dated 1713, in possession of Donovan family, Ballymore, County Wexford, no pagination.

Price, Rebecca. 1974. *The Compleat Cook, or the Secrets of a Seventeenth Century Housewife, compiled and introduced by Madeleine Masson*. London: Routledge and Kegan Paul. 0710074441

Riviere, Lazare. 2005. *Six Hundred Miseries; the Seventeenth Century Womb, Book 15 of the Practice of Physick*. Translated by Nicholas Culpeper and published in London in 1698. Edited by John L Burton. London: RCOG Press. 1904752136

Stapley, Christina. 2004. *The Receipt Book of Lady Ann Blencowe. Seventeenth Century Cookery and Home Medicine*. Basingstoke: Heartsease. 0952233657

Spurlig, Hilary. 1986. *Elinor Fettiplace's Receipt Book: Elizabethan Country House Cooking*. London: Viking Salamander. 0948681039

Quarton, Margorie (ed). 2010. *Mary Cannon's Commonplace Book*. Dublin: Lilliput Press. 9781843511854

Twigge, Diana. *Recipe Book of Diana Twigge*. National Archives of Ireland, M. 6231

Wilson, Anne. 1973. *Waterford Chronicle. (No.722) 1776*

Woolley, Hannah. 1988. *The Recipes of Hannah Woolley. English Cookery of the Seventeenth Century. Edited for Today's Cooks and Introduced by Matthew Hamlyn*. [s.l.]: Heineman Kingswood. 0434981028

Editor's Note

I first saw Hannah Alexander's recipe book the summer just after I had handed in my PhD thesis, in 1997. My mother explained that it had been at the back of a drawer all this time; the last additions to the book had been made about 250 years before. We are a family of hoarders and, while this has its drawbacks, sometimes it pays off. Among the tins containing carefully stored baby teeth that once belonged to ancestors who have long since grown old and died, Hannah's book had been waiting.

The timing of my personal discovery of the handwritten recipe book was good, as I had a few weeks with nothing to do, so I laboriously transcribed the document, puzzling over the handwriting and thinking what fun it would be if we could publish it one day.

You might think that a recipe book wouldn't reveal much about the author, but as I transcribed it seemed very clear to me that it had been written by someone who really enjoyed food. Hannah must have obtained these recipes from friends and family and from diverse printed sources, but they seem to have an individual touch; they are written in a conversational style and it's easy to imagine two women sitting in a kitchen together sharing recipes and secret ingredients. Some of the recipes are lengthy and detailed and others contain the impatient suggestion that the dish be cooked "until it is enough". I imagined Hannah or her daughter Hannah Dorothea getting bored of writing and rushing back to her kitchen to whip up one of her pyes or hashes or puddings.

The medical section of the book, while interesting, doesn't have the same conversational tone as the cookery section and wasn't as much fun to transcribe. I presume that Hannah and Hannah Dorothea simply copied the medical receipts from published sources; the fact that they were able to use "guide words" (putting the first word of the recipe on the following page in the bottom right hand corner) suggests that this was the case. Hopefully they did not often have to use the remedies, which sometimes seem almost as bad as the illnesses they are supposed to cure, often involving ingredients such as the lungs of a fox, fresh from the fox ("For Shortness of Breath", p. 143) or escalating quantities of juice obtained by squeezing millipedes or wood lice ("For Ulcers in the Breast and Elswhere", p. 121).

Having grown up in Ireland in the 1970s and 80s, I was very surprised by the wealth and diversity of the ingredients Hannah used, many of which I had never heard of in a culinary context before, if at all. Hannah is an ancestor of ours and we know that the family was relatively comfortably off—far below the gentry but wealthier than most people in Ireland at the time. They evidently had enough money to produce the rich foods described here. Even still, thinking about Irish kitchens filled with such exotic ingredients as anchovies and nutmeg, mace and ambergris, was a big surprise. I started to try out some of the recipes and found that many are absolutely delicious, if not exactly cut out for anyone on a weight loss diet. It seems that Ireland's food culture, at least among the middle classes, was once much more rich and varied than most of us would have imagined. Potatoes hardly get a mention.

By the time I had finished the initial transcript and printed out a copy, I had other things to do. Hannah's recipe book—now in both its digital and its hand-written versions—returned to the back of a drawer until 2013, when work was resumed on the document prior to its publication. 2013 was also the year when Jennifer Nuttall, Hannah's many-times-great-niece, wrote a BA thesis on the recipe book, providing us with the historical information that forms the introduction to this volume.

From its beginnings in the late seventeenth century to 2014, when Ireland has finally started to embrace its culinary heritage, is a long time to wait, but it is very exciting to know that Hannah's book, which she wrote with such care and love, is finally being published, having been beautifully typeset by Michael Everson of Evertype in contemporary Caslon with a titling font that is evocative of Hannah's own script, albeit much easier to read. Entirely by coincidence, I now live just a 10-minute stroll away from the location of Hannah's house on Ship Street in Dublin (the house is gone; the site is now occupied by the nether regions of the Radisson Hotel, but a neighbouring house on the same street is featured on the back cover of this book). I often walk into town that way and wonder how Hannah would have felt if she had known that her book would be published more than three hundred years after she started it.

Deirdre Nuttall

Acknowledgements

Many thanks to everyone who assisted with this project, especially Margaret Donovan of Ballymore Farm Features, Camolin, for permission to read Mary Ogle's Commonplace Book recipe book and other farm books of the eighteenth century; Sylvia Reynolds for her botanical expertise; Nicholas Williams for his knowledge of botanical terms; and John and Elinor Medlycott for the loan of a contemporary copy of Edward Kidder's receipt book. Thanks also to the staff at the National Archive for assistance with research and to the New Ross library for help in sourcing reference books.

Above all, thanks to our family and friends for interest and encouragement. Particular thanks to Brian Nuttall, who has not complained of living with the Alexanders of the past as well as the present, and to the many people who have partaken in meals prepared using this Book of Cookery.

Deirdre Nuttall

Jennifer Nuttall *née* Alexander

A Book of Cookery

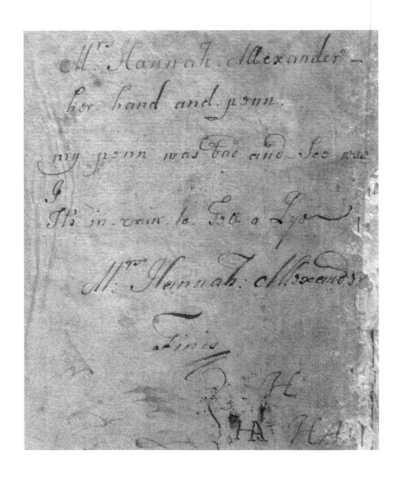

Mrs Hannah Alexander—
her hand and penn

my penn was bad and Soe was I;
It's in vain to Tell a Lye

Explanacon

An Explanacon of severall hard wordes that you will meet with in the following books of cookery and phisical receipts:

A **vehicle** is a convenieant quantity of liquor for the better of boiling down of any physick that you may not be efforted with that after.

Reitrate is to do a thing over again, as to repeat a thing in the very same.

Bolus is a thick substance to roll up in a ball.

Subtile is well done or ground or beaten.

Incorporat is to mix severall things so well together to be as one thing.

A **mass** is severall compounds made up in one lump.

A **poultis** is herbs or roots stamped to a thick substance as to be madding with oyle or water

Amulet is a ball made up like pomander or a thing to hang about the neck.

Impregnation is a thing made so strong that it cannot be forced away.

Hiltow, is to strain through a woollen cloath or any other cloath or through a sieve

A **Cattaplasm** is a medium or poultis made of herbs etc.

PART I

1

Soups

To make a Crawfish soope

First you must make an Onion Broath. W[th] this done take some Onions and slyce them as you think fitt and frye them in butter, and when they are brown putt to them hott water and boyle them well with a sprigg of tyme, a little pepper. Then take toasts and putt them in a dish and poure some of this broath over them and season it with salt, then beate 2 yolks of eggs with some verjuice and put it to that, which is to whiten it, than take a carpe and slyce thin and take out the bones and mince the fish very small with some parsely and some chobles, then take a piece of white bread and soake it in the broath, so squeez it and put it to the carpe with a quarter of a pound of butter and season it with pepper and salt and when it is well minct take halfe of it, and set it a stewing with a little broath, then put 2 yolks of eggs to the rest and worke it together and take little of it to make balls and save the rest to stuff the bodys of the crawfish and take the rest of the Crawfish and pound them in a mortar and strain them with a little broath, so set them aside, then take a little butter and set it over the fire and when it is hott pour in the stufft bodyes with the fish side downwards to make it brown. Then putt in the broath of the pounded Crawfish with a little dust of pepper, salt, a sprigg of time, with halfe a white Onion, and a bitt of Lemon, and let them stew till they are enough, then take another saucepann, and put in it a piece of butter and set it over the fire wth mushrooms and let them stew a whyle, then take boyled Hartechocks and put in the bottoms of 2 or 3 with the balls, the meate of the carpe cutt in peeces, then put broath to them and let them stew a while with halfe a white Onyon, a sprigg of time, 3 Cloves, a bitt of lemon with a little pepper, and salt, then cover it and Let it stew till it is enough and thicken it with a little butter. So sett it by, then take toasts as you think fitt and putt them in the dish you design for the table, and set it over the fire, and let them stew very well, then take the stewed craw that was stewed by it selfe and lay it thin over the bread, and garnish it with the stufft bodyes and pour your liqour over them, and lay of the Ragou and squize some lemon over it.

To make an Excellent Soupe

Take 2 leggs of Beefe, let them stew all night over the fire, then take it and strayn it, and set it to coole, then take of the fatt and lett it over a slow fire with some grass pepper, mace and cloves, some grated bread, as much salt as will season it, if you please you may thicken it with some pease boyled very soft, and strained, then take some loaves of french bread and lay in your dish then take it off the spitt, slash it do not cutt it in pieces and boyle it in your soope. This broath will make a ffrench potage, only adding a good handfull of Lettice, as much spinach, as much fennel, as much beets, a faggott of sweet herbs, do not cutt the tender herbs, you make another sorte of potage by putting in carrots, cabbidge, turnips, parsnips, small shred and a piece of butter.

To make a Peas soope
Take good pease and boyle them all to pieces, take them and strayn them. Then take some strong broath & Gravey, as much of the one as the other, then take some forced balls of either veal or beefe suet and some grated bread, and put in an egg or two, and season it well with Sweet Spices, and a small quantity of salt & worke it stiffe and make it into balls some lesser and some bigger and frye them in butter. Then season your soope with a litle sweet spice, then dish your soop and putt in your balls, some whole and some broken, then shake your soop together and serve it up.

To Boyle Brawne
When your brawne is bound and cutt into square pieces cast some salt upon it, and bind it up with Course tape as hard as you can possible and boyle it and when it is tender as you may thread a straw through it take it up and cast some salt upon it and

when it is cold put it into soupe as you may make of taplash or brawne boyled in water and strayn it, it makes good soupe.

To make a Soop

Take 2 quarts of strong broath, 2 balls of forced meat, a white Loafe cutt in Slices and together with a Ladle full of gravy and a handful of spinnage, then roast a duck and Lard it with Bacon and putt it in the midle of the dish and so serve it up.

The best Pottage

Take strong Broath seasoned with sweet herbs & spice, thickened with french roll then put it in a Capon, sweet breads, palletts, Lambs tongues, sheepe tongues, Cabbadge leaves, Hawthorne bottoms, all these boyled till they be very tender, & sent up in order.

Biskett Pottage

Take a Legg of Beefe, and beat it all to pieces, and make very good strong broth of it, take a duck and five pidgeons, and halfe rost them, put them into the strong broth, and boyle them in it, have ready some sweetbread and pullatts & Cocks combs stood in a little pipkin with a few Cloves, mace, and a little grated bread well rasped, put it in a dish, and poure in some strong broath in it, and let it boyle upon a token of Coals till it be very soft and till the Liquor be all boyled away that it may stick on the bottom of the dish and not swinge on the top, so place all your meat on the dish and poure on the broath it being seasoned with salt and so send it away.

2

Meat Dishes

To make a Cold hash

Take veale and mince it wth horsradish, Chives, Lemon and Anchovies and Onyon pepper, and Capers, you may do Turkey, Capon or Pullot the same way.

To hash a Calves head

Take a calves head, parboyle it, then take one side of it, and cutt off the flesh from the bone in pieces the bigness of your thumb, season it wth salt, mace, cloves, pepper, put in some oysters and capers, and let it stew over a slow fire, take a little white wine and anchovies & the liquor of your hash and thicken it with the yolks of 6 Eggs, put it into your stew pann to your meat and let it just heate with the fire, then shake it well till you see it thick, then carbonade the other side of the head. Lay it in the middle of the dish and pour the meat over it, do not forgett when it is stewing to putt in a faggott of sweet herbs, a shallott, a lemon. You might garnish your dish with french balls which you make of any sort of raw meat being small sliced with as much suet as meat, some mace, cloves, pepper and salt, some sweet herbs, some sweet marjoram, some paste, and make it up into balls, either frye them or boyle them, garnish your dish with pickles.

❧

To hash a Calves head (2)

Take your Calves head and boyle it very well, take it out when t'is boyled and let it stand till it be cold, and when it is cold take out the bones and slyce it in very thin slyces, then take a stew pan and put your meat in with some strong broth that is made with a knuckle of veale and a legg of beef till it be boyled to a jelly, then take some of that and putt it into your hash, and stew it very well. Take some beaten Cloves and some nutmeg and a small quantity of salt, and season your hash, then take some large oysters and drayn them but a little, then take some good Capers and mince them very small, and put them into your hash, then take 2 or 3 yolks of eggs and breake them in white wine, and put them in to your hash, and shake them together till they go to thick and dish them and lay your oysters as you think fitt upon your hash, and a little grated bread and an egg together and so garnish the brims of your dish.

❧

To hash a Calves head another way

Take a Calves head and parboyle it. Cutt all the flesh from the bones of one side of it and putt it into a

Sauce pan with some strong broath, some Cloves, mace, and some grass pepper, a faggott of sweet herbs, a handfull of oysters, as much capers cutt small, and putt in then two shallotts small cut. Let this stew very well together over the fire an houre and a half then Carbonade the other halfe of the head and boyle it, and putt it in the midle of the dish, when it is ready to poure all the liquor from your meate into a skillett with some white wine and Anchovies and beate the yolks of 4 eggs and shake over the fire to keep it from Curdling, then poure it into the stew pan where your meate is, and shake it two or three times, then poure it into your dish, it being garnished with grated bread, and forced balls, which you may make of any sorte of meate you have in the house and shred it small with as much suett as meate, a handfull of sweet herbs, some pepper, salt, cloves and mace and 2 eggs, then roull them up in Balls, and either broyle them or frye them. You may garnish with Collops or fryed Goose with those balls.

To hash Cold Ducks and other foule

Take your Ducks and cut them very small, then put them into a stew pan with some strong broth and put them over the fire slowly stewing and so that they do not burne. Take a shallot and 2 or 3 Anchovies and a mushroom, mince them small and put them into your stew pan, with a little Cloves and Mace, then take a little Gravy and a little Claret wine, so let it boyle together and dish it up.

To make Courtletts

Take a neck of mutton, boyle it and cutt it assunder, the bones severally, then Season it with pepper, salt, cloves, mace, Nuttmegg minced, parsely & grated bread, then frye it in butter brown, then clear off all the butter and putt in a pinte of white wine, a glass of ale, 2 shallotts, 2 Anchovies, the yolks of 2 Eggs beaten very well, putt the eggs in just as you take the pann off the fire and so serve them.

For a dish of Cuttletts

Take a large Neck of Mutton and cutt it into small stakes, beate them flatt, take a good handfull of parsley and shredd it very small, then take a handfull of salt and grated bread, and a little flower, mix them altogether, and slap it on the stakes upon both sides and broyle them browne upon a clear fire. Then take a little strong broath, a little Gravey and little broken cloves and mace, 2 or 3 Anchovies, a shallot and mix together, boyle them up together with gravy also and so serve them up.

To Collar Beefe

Take a plate of beefe, bone it and skin it, then season it with salt and saltpeter and let it lye 24 hours or more then take it up and season it with mace, cloves and pepper, two handfulls of sweet herbes cutt small and rubb it in the side of your meat, with a shallott cutt small. Then roule it up harde as you can and bind it

To Collar Beefe

Take a plate of Beefe, bone it, skin it,
season it well with salt and saltpeter,
Let it Lye in that 4 dayes, then take
it and season it with pepper, mace & cloves
a hand full of sweet herbes small cutt
with a shallott, then Roll it up hard and
tye it with a tape, and put it in the
pott you will bake it in with 3 quarts
of pump water and a quart of
clarett, Cover your pot with paper
sett it in the oven with brown bread
when you draw it take it out of
the Liquor, keep it dry, and when
you serve it to the table take off
the tape and serve it up with
Vineger

hard with Course Tape, then putt it into a pott that will contain it together with three quarts of pump water, and a quart of Clarett, cover your pott, Close with paper and paste, and sett it into your oven, with houshold bread, and let it stand all night, then take it out of the liquor, and let it dry, and serve it up.

To Collar Beefe (2)

Take a plate of Beefe, bone it, skin it, season it well with salt and saltpeter. Let it Lye in that 4 days, then take it and season it with pepper, mace & cloves, a handful of sweet herbes small cutt with a shallott, then Roll it up hard and tye it with a tape and putt it in the pott. You will bake it in wth 3 quarts of pump water and a quart of Clarett, Cover your pot wth paper, sett it in the oven with brown bread. When you draw it, take it out of the Liquor, keep it dry and when you serve it to the table take off the tape and serve it up with vinegar.

To Bake Beefe red deer fashion

Take a phillott of Beefe, put it in a coarse Cloath and beate it with a wooden pestell then Lay it to steep in Clarott wine 24 houres, then take it out and season it with Ginger, Nuttmegg, Mace, Pepper with a good deale of salt, then lay it a little while in a light press, then take it forth and Lard it with the fatt of porke or Baccon, and so put it in a Coarse paste with about a

pound of butter, bake it thorrowly, and when it is
almost cold fill it up with melted butter.

To Pott Beefe like Vennison

Take some of a haunch and cutt it in thin slyces.
Beate it well with a Rolling pin, season it well with
saltpetre, an ounce of pepper, and as much Nuttmegg, then lay it in the pott you will bake it in, and
between every layer of beefe cover it with suett small
cutt then bake it, let your meat lye very close in your
pott, and cover your pott with paper.

To Stew a Rumpe of Beefe

Parboyle it halfe, then take it up in a dish, and cutt it
of the inside that the Gravie may run out, then strew
of pepper and salt in these cutts, and fill the dish with
good Claret wine, and putt in 3 or 4 blades of mace,
and cover it close, and put it on the coals to stew an
houre and a halfe often stirring, and take off the fatt.

Beefe Allamode

Take a Buttock of Beefe, and take out all the strings
& Sinnews & fatt, cutt it in slices and beat it well in
a Mortar, then lay it in the same pickle you do
Collared beefe, then season it with 3 quarters of an
ounce of Nuttmegg, halfe an ounce of Cloves, as
much Mace, half a pound of fatt Baccon, putt this in

a pott and cover it with paper and bake it 3 hours and when it is baked cleare out all the liquor, and melt as much butter as will cover it, so cutt it out for your use.

Balls of Veale or Mutton

Take a piece of the ffillett of veale or legg of mutton, and mince it small with pennyroyall & parsley, mix it with some grated bread, Currants, Cloves, pepper and salt and beaten Eggs, make them up like balls, crush them with your hand & boyle them in a deep dish on a chaffing dish of coulor wth some water or a mutton broath with currants, butter & barberrys and sprinkle some Rosewater on your sippets and thus garnish your dish.

To doe Beefe Collops

Take the phillott of Beefe, out of the Surloyne, or out of the tenderest of buttuck, and slyce it in very thin Collops, beate them very well with the back of a knife, season them wth pepper and salt and frye them in pure Clarified butter, and when they are fryed put away the Liquour from them and power into them hafe a pinte of Gravey, a little Clarett wine, some Savory, Time & Parsely, minced very small, an onion stuck wth cloves, 2 Anchovies, a quarter of a pound of butter, a little Lemon pill very small and the juyce of a Lemon, halfe a Nuttmegg grated, and the crust of a ffrench Roull grated or the yolks of two eggs which you please you may thicken it and give it a quick heate over the fire tossing it still up, have your dish Garnished with Lemon and dish it wth Sippetts and send it away.

To make Scotch Collops

Take a Legg of veale and cutt some of it in thin slyces, and Lard some of it with Baccon, and beate it well with the back of your knife, season it with mace, Cloves, pepper and salt, then putt it into a frying pan with some water, and sett it over the fire till it is tender, then poure out the Liquor, and put in a piece of fresh butter, and frye them browne, then take the Liquor you poured from them and put in a little wine and Anchovies and thicken it with the yolks of 4 eggs, then put your meat into your dish and putt your liqour all over it and serve it up.

Scotch Collops

Take a very fatt neck of Mutton, cutt it into stakes, and beat it very thin and Lay them all broad one by one. Wash them all over with Gravey and sprinkle all over with minced sweet herbs and salt, broyle them with a very quick fire. Have for your sauce some very good Gravy & Anchovie, the tender parts of 6 oysters bruised so small as you can not see any of them whole, a little sweet herbs and a little lemon pill minced very small, a little nutmegg, a little bit of fresh butter and a little Clarett wine, and give it a boyle on a token of coals, keeping it still stirring that it may be thick, dish your collops and send them away, you must send them after the rest of your meate, for if they be not eaten very hott they will not be the same thing.

❦

To fforce a Legg of Mutton

Take a Legg of mutton & cutt all the flesh of the shin, but be sure you cutt not the skin, then take the flesh and shredd it small, with as much suett as meate, then season it with cloves, mace, nuttmegg, salt and pepper and a handfull of sweet herbs, 2 shallotts, one handfull of oysters, a handfull of capers, 3 Eggs. Shredd all these together very well, mix it with eggs like paste then fill the skin, and cover the Lapp of mutton over, and tye it up in a cloathe, and boyle it. Save some of the mince meate to make balls to Garnish the dish, then make some sauce with gravy and oysters & capers and some butter drawn thick, and poure all over the mutton, you may putt boyled Chickens about it if you please.

❦

To Ragoo a Breast of Veale

Take a Legg of veale and boyle it down for strong broath, get some Leen beefe and make some Gravy asunder til you are ready to serve it up, Rost your breast of veale, and stew it in your strong broath, after you have taken the bones from the broath, and season it with a little spices, as cloves, mace and a little quantity of salt, and just before you serve it up put in your Gravy, and shake it together 2 or 3 times, your dish being garnished with a little bread, and throw 2 or 3 forsed balls, & so serve it up.

To Ragoo a Westphalia Ham

Take a Ham and boyle it very well, and when it is neare boyled take it out, and put it into a large saucepan, and put it over the fire, with some fresh Liqour to keep it hott over a Charcoale fire and just before you serve it up put it into strong broath as before and use the Gravey as before with 2 or 3 boyled pidgeons about it, and season your broath as before. According to the pallat you may take a little pease broath and strain it and so serve it up.

To Collar Pigg

Take a pigg of 3 weeks old, and when it is clean cutt off the head and cleave it down the back and bone it, season it with salt, mace and Cloves, a little pepper, a little Sage, Roll it up, tye it with a tape, then tye it in a Cloath, and boyle it in water and salt, till it be so tender you may put a straw throw it, then take off the cloath and put in the Liquor that was boyled in a pint of vinegar and two lemons, cutt it thin slyces, some bay Leaves, some whole mace, some gras pepper, when cold put in your Collars. It will be fitt to eate in three days.

To Collar Pigg (2)

Take a pigg of about 3 weeks old. Lett it be very fat and when it is hung Cleave down the back then bone it and season it with some mace, cloves and some figs small cutt, a little pepper and salt, then roll it up hard and tye it with tape, then sow it in a Cloath, then boyle it with water and salt to when that you may throw it then take the cloath from about it, but not the tape, and boyle the water that it was boyled in. Put in some Vinegar with lemon cut in thin slices, some eggs in pieces and let all boyle together, take it off the fire and when it is cold put the Collars & cover it and it will be fit to eat in a weeke.

To make sassages

Take 2 pound of filletts and a pound and a half of hoggs suet, and half a pound of hoofs, shredd very small, & a handfull of salt and pepper together and more salt than pepper & 3 handfulls of sage.

To make a Porridg

Take a pullott and roast it, and take some strong broath and stew it up as before and just before you serve it up put in your Gravy and a little grated bread and shake it together, take a pinte of boyled milke and take the porridge off the fire and put the milke to it before it Coole, dish it up and serve it, Let your dish be Garnished among potting Vennyson or Beefe.

To make a made dish

Take some of the Legg of Lambe, and the weight of
it in suett, some sweet herbs, & mince together and
take some sugar, mace, cloves & some salt, two or
three Eggs, some grated bread, Rose water at the
bottom of your dish, and lay the meat in the dish in
layers and take some marrow and Lay on the top and
some sweet butter on that and cover your meate and
dish up, puffe paste and so bake it, take a little verjuis
and sweet butter and sugar for a caudle and draw it up
thick, and when the dish comes out of the oven cutt
a little hole in it and poure it in and so serve it up.

To make a dish of tripes and puffe

Take your tripes out of the source and squees them
and dry them, then take some flower and Eggs and
make batter of it, putt in a little cloves & mace fryed,
suett rendered very well and putt in a frying pan,
make your liqour very hott and dipp your tripes in to
your butter and putt them into y^r hott liqour then frye
them, then melt some butter very thick and put some
mustard into your butter, and serve it up.

To Make peas porridge

Take a shin or Legg of beefe, or any other knuckles of
meate that will make strong broath, and a quart of
pease, Let it boyle till the peas and the meat is all
boyled to pieces, then strain it out through a hair sieve
then take violet leaves, spinnage & strawberry &

sweet marjoram, and sorrell, but you might put in that to be but just scalded, and mace and white pepper and the bottom of manshott, to lay in the middle, a boyled capon, or pullott by itself with slyces of bacon. This way you make green pease porridge, only put in your pease when you put in your hearbes.

Boyle Magott Poridge
Take a henn and Boyle with strong jelly broath and tosted sippetts layd in the bottom, and when the broath is ready to take up, putt in the magotts and Lay them all upon the henn.

To Maullolet a young Rabbitt
Take your rabbitts and cutt them in pieces. Crack the bones and wash them, then sqeez them, and putt them into a frying pan, and putt in some strong broath in them, then take a little parsely, and a little sorrell, an Onyon or a shallot, mince them and put them in the pan, and put a little pepper and salt and a little cloves and mace to season them, then take the 2 yolks of eggs, and beate them with a little claret wine, then take a little sweet butter and put into your pan, toss them together til they be pretty thick but see they do not Curdle and so serve them up.

To Fry Chickens & Rabbits

Take 3 or 4 Chickens or Rabbits, little
ones about the bigness of a partridge are
best, boyle them till they be half enough
then take them and cutt them into peeces
like a hash, sett them a stewing in some strong
broath, season it with pepper and salt
& some lemon pill, when it is stewed very
tender putt it into a fryeing pan and
let it stand over the fire a while, then
have 2 or 3 yelks of eggs and a good
peece of butter melted, and some parsley
scalded and shredd, nuttmegg and juyce
of lemon good store, power this over your
Chickens in the pann, shake them
all togeather, and so dish it and
serve it up

To Boyle Rabbits the French way

Take your Rabbits and truss them flying way, take the livers and a handfull of sippets, a handfull of fennall and a litle tyme, mince them small altogether with an Anchovie beaten small mixed with pepper, and the yolks of 2 eggs and put it in the Rabbits Belly and boyle them in halfe white wine & water, and a little salt. For your sauce take a pound of fresh butter and an Anchovie and the juice of a lemon or two, a little pepper, and Nuttmegg, a quarter of a pinte of Gravy, 2 yolks of hard eggs very small, beate these alltogether very thick, when you take up the Rabbits, put all the stuffing to the sauce, and stirr it altogether. If it be very thick put the yolke of one raw egg to it. Garnish your dish with Lemon and Scalded Spinnage, and dish up the Rabbits and poure on the sauce and send it away.

To Fry Chickens & Rabbits

Take 3 or 4 Chickens or Rabbitts, like ones about the bignes of a partridge are best, boyle them till they be half enough, then take them and cutt them into peeces like a hash, sett this a-stewing in some strong broth, season it with pepper and salt & some Lemon pill, when it's stewed very tender putt it into a fryeing pan and Let it stand over the fire a while, then have 2 or 3 yolks of Eggs and a good peece of butter melted, and some parsley scalded and shredd, Nuttmegg and juyce of Lemon, a good slew, poure this over your Chickens in the pann, shake them all together, and so dish it and serve it up.

To Boyle Chickins

Take a little water and putt it to a little oatmeal, and a blade of mace then season it with salt. When your water boyles put in your Chickens, then take a little lettice and boyle it in water and salt & mace, when it is tender strew them in butter and verjuice and sugar & Grapes or Gooseberrys and beate them together and poure them on the Chickens with sippets wth a little lemon and bayberrys.

To Make a frigicce of rabits or Chickins

Take 2 or 3 young Rabits & cut um in Litle pieces & fry them with a little bit of buter keeping um stirring till they are almost Enough. Then put to them a pint of Strong broath or fair water, half a pint of Clarit, a little peper & Salt, Nutmeg, long Mace, a bunch of Sweet herbs, a shelot or a bit of Onyon, let it stew till it is tender then add to it an Anchovi Minc'd Small with a sprig of time, a few Capers, a little vinigar. Thicken it with a little burnt buter & an egg, then put some whole capers, mushrooms, forced Meat Balls. Shake them all together, and put it in a Dish with Sipits, Some fried, with parsly Dipt in Eggs. Garnish it with Slicd lemon. When you make it of Chickens, leave out the Claret & put white wine instead of it.

For a ffriccacie

Take Chickens or Rabbits and quarter them, breake the bones very well and let them boyle in a little

Liquor and put them into a frying pan with some of the same Liquor and take a shallott or an Union, and a little parsley, and mix them very small, and strew them into your frying pan, then take Cloves and mace beaten, a small quantity of salt, and mix them altogether and so season your meate in the pan, shake it in the pan over the fire, take some sweet butter and wash it, take some sweet breads, and beate 2 or 3 Eggs with a little flower, and so dipp your sweet breads into your butter with some drippings into another pan and make the Liqour hott, and so put in your sweetbreads and frye them brown, and take some great oysters and do them in the same way as you did the sweet breads and fry them. Take 2 or 3 Eggs, and beate them with a Glass of clarett, then putt your butter into the pann, and afterwards putt in the Eggs and wine and shake them well together till they grow thick, and put them into your dish, here a sweetbread and there an oyster as your fancy pleaseth, and grate a crust of bread round your dish and so serve it up.

To make white Puddings

Take a couple of pullotts and roast them and take the white part of them and mince it very small, then take two pounds of Lard, and mince likewise and mix them together and season them with pepper and salt, and a little Anniseeds beaten with the crums of 2 Roules and sett a pinte of milke a boyling with a white onyon cutt in pieces, then whipp two Eggs very well and strain the milke to them and putt to the meate, so worke them well together and fill them in Sheeps gutts then take milke and water and set it over the fire and let it boyle, then putt in your puddings and when they boyle take them off and cover them Close, keeping them under liqour, and let them lye till they are cold, those are to be broyled and eaten with mustard.

A haggish

Take the lights, hearte and kidneys of a Lamb or sheep but not the Liver. Boyle them and pick out the strings, mince them small with a good slew of beef suet mingled with Currans, nutmeg, salt and grated bread and sweet meat shred small, 3 yolks of Eggs, 4 spoonfulls of cream. Stirr them together and put them into the paunch of a sheep stowed and seasoned for 2 or 3 days together. Let it boyle 4 hours then take it up and stirr it in the paunch and cut it a gash carefully and it will run out green.

Liver Puddings

Take a hoggs liver and boyle it overnight. Next morning cutt off the outside and beate it in a mortar, mingle it with Cream as you beate it. When it is finely beaten put it into a hair sieve, then rubb it through with your hand, putting Cream to it if it be too stiffe. Mingle with it a good quantity of grated bread, a quart of Cream, 2 pound of currants, 2 rootes of Ginger beaten, the yolks of 12 eggs, as much beefe sewitt as will make them very fatt then fill the Gutts and boyle them.

ᘰᘓ✿ᘔᘱ

Liver pudding

Take a good piece of hogs liver parboyled, sweet marjoram, Thyme, pennyroyal and winter savory, of each a good quantity. Wash them and grind them well, put into them some sweet Cream & strain them together with grated bread, 4 yolks and one whole Egg just shred small, season it with salt, brown cloves, nutmegg, cinnamon and sugar, fill the skins and boyle them.

ᘰᘓ✿ᘔᘱ

Liver Pudding (2)

Take a good piece of hogs liver parboiled, sweet marjoram, Thyme, Pennyroyall and winter savory, of each a good quantity. Wash them, and ground them well, put to them some sweet cream, and strain them together, grated bread, 4 yolks, and one white of egg, beef suet shred small, currents washt and rubd. Season it with salt, Beaten cloves, Nuttmegg Cinnamon and Sugar, fill the skins and then boyle them.

ᘰᘓ✿ᘔᘱ

Calves feet Pudding

Mince the meat of 2 Calves feet with the crums of 2 penny loaves very small, half a pound of Beefe suet,

5 Eggs and a handfull of currants, grated bread, Nuttmeg and sugar, with what other spice you please, put it into a Caule of veale sowed up like a bagg, put in good slew of marrow in great peeces, put it in up in a napkin and then into boyling water for 2 hours, stick it full of blanched almonds cutt in quarters, make sauce of sweet butter, verjuice and sugar, you may scalld your bread in a quart of cream and then leave out 5 Eggs.

3

Sauces to Accompany Meats

To make Gravie
Take some bacon and cutt it into thin Slyces, and lay
it on the bottom of a slow pann in slices as you cutt it
side by side, then take an Onyon and stick some
cloves in it, with a sprigg of tyme, and a few sweet
herbs tyed in a bunch, and take a pound of Beefe, and
cut it likewise in thin slyces, and Lay it over the
bacon. So lett it frye till it begines to burn to the
bottom of the stew pan, and you must be sure to keep
stirring it, and squeezing it till you think the juice is
out of it, then put to it 5 or 6 Ladles of beefe broath,
and let it boyle very well together.

Sauce for all sorts of wild foule
Take a peece of Lean beefe, Carbonade it on one
side, and flower the other. Lay the flower side to the
pann, then fry it in butter the biggnes of an Egg, let
it frye up to the top of the pann, then add a glass of
Clarett, a ladlefull of strong broath, 2 Anchovies, a
Nuttmegg quartered, a blade of Mace, 2 shallotts, a

bunch of sweet herbs. Let all those boyle together till it is enough, then poure this through the foule just as you dish them.

4

Fish Dishes

To Collar Eeles

Take the Largest Eels you can get. Slitt them down
the body and take out the backbone, season it with
mace, cloves and pepper, salt, a little sage small cutt,
then roll them up. Bind them with tape, put them in
water and salt, let the water boyle before you putt
them in, when boyled take them up, and put some
white wine in the Liquor, and lemon cutt in thin
slices, a little grass pepper, whole mace, when they
are cold put them together. If you will have them to
eat the next day then put in vinegar instead of white
wine.

To Collar Eeles (2)

Take the Largest Eels and slitt them down the Belly.
Take out the back bone and then season them with
cloves, mace and pepper, then Roull them up and tye
them, cast them into water and salt and a quantity of
white wine, and 2 lemons, slyce them, and putt in a
handfull of Bay leaves and when they are boyld

enough take them up, and lett them Coole. After let the liquor coole, when they are thoroughly cold putt them together, you may soupe any fish but makerall and then you may putt sweet herbs in the sause.

To stew Eeles

Take six Eels and bone then. Roule them, season them with mace, Nuttmeg, salt and pepper, then putt them into a saucepan with half a pinte of white wine, a glass of vinegar, some whole peppers. Let them stew together until they are enough. Dissolve one Anchovie in the same liquor, and a few sweet herbs. Garnish your dish with herbs and pieces of eel fried.

A friccasee of Oysters

Take a quart of the best Oysters and put them in a frying pan with some white wine and their own Liquor, and little salt and some whole spice, and 2 or 3 Bay leaves, when you think they are enough Lay them in a dish well warmed, then mix with your Liquor 2 Anchovies, some butter and the yolks of 4 Eggs, put some sippets about the dish and serve it up.

To Boyle a Pike ye french way

Take the pike and Garbush & Scale it. Cutt the chinebone cleare out, put it in a deep dish, take a quart or three pints of vinegar as your pike is in bigness boyle them with salt and poure it boyling hott on the pike, Let it Lye in it 3 houres. Boyle it with salt and water and the Liqour it was soaked in and a Lemon pill, when it is boyled drayn the water well from it and dish it, have for your sauce a pound of fresh butter beaten and good store of Horse Raddish scraped very small, 3 rootes of Ginger, the Juice of a Lemon, two spoonfulls of Gravey, beaten well together, and thickened with the yolk of an egg and poure it upon the pike, haveing fixed tosts in the bottom of the dish and Garnished with lemons and send it away.

To dish a Cods head

When the Cods head is boyled in water and salt and lemon and sweet herbs then take a pint of white wine, 2 Anchovies. Add the juice of Lemon, some capers, a blade of mace, half a nutmeg, a few barberrys, a pint of Oysters. Sett this over the fire till the Anchovies be dissolved. Putt into the Liquor two pound of butter, 2 yolks of eggs. Pour all this over the head, then stick it of the small bones. Putt on top some oysters, shrimps and sliced lemon, then garnish the dish with fryed fish, forced fish, Burberrys, lemon pill and capers.

5
Sauces for Fish

Sauce for a Cods head

Take mace, cloves and Grass pepper and boyle it in halfe a pinte of white wine till it is halfe consumed then put it in an earthen vessel or sauce pan, strew some oysters, some Cockles, some Capers, a little Anchovies, horse Rhaddish, then draw a pound of butter thick and putt it into your oysters and the other things and the wyne, and a lemon cutt small, when your dish is well drest poure your sauce over it, and garnish your dish with some of the pease of the cod fryed brown and some small fishes as trowts, or whiteings dipt in butter made with eggs fryed and set round your dish. Garnish the brimms of your dish with any sorte of pickled sallatt and Bayberrys.

6

Preserved, Bottled, and Dried Meats

To Salt Neats Tongues

Take as many as you please, salt them for 5 or 6 days then throw the bloody brine away, and take as much white as bay salt and salt them well again, then take 2 ounces of salt peter, pound it, and strew it all over the tongues, and so let them lye in a tubb a forthnight or three weeks, then take them out and boyle y^r brine, and add as much salt and water as will cover it, and boyle it till it be so strong to bear an egg, and when it is cold putt your tongues in and putt them in an earthen pott, and so they will keep all the yeare, but it is exceeding good to boyle your brine once a month.

To dry Hams

To each ham an ounce of salt peter and some bay salt, and white, let them lye a forthnight on each side, then

smoake them in a Chimny that burns turfe or sawdust, they must be kept a yeare.

To dry Neats Tongues or Gamon of Baccon

Take well or pump water that makes meat red, make
a strong bryne with bay salt and boyle it until it will
beare an Egg. After it hath stood all night and is well
cleared putt in the tongues and Let them Lye 3
weeks every day turning them about, then take them
out and wipe them with a Cloath, and rub them with
a little bran, so putt strings into the end of them, and
hang them up in a roome where there is moderate
heate, hang them in a Chimney, then smoake them
with wett hay 3 or 4 days then take them down and
hang them where they might be kept dry, thus you
may do Gamons, but they must lye a forthnight longer
in the Brine.

How to pott all sorts of foule that are to be baked

Take a Goose and bone it, season the flesh very well
with pepper and and a little Nuttmegg and Lay them
in your pan with some butter, and when it is very well
baked squeez out all the Liquor, and when the meat
is dry, putt it in the pott and cover it with melted
butter. When your pott is cold Cover it Close from
aire, as for small fowle take off the Leggs & heads and
push down flatt. Crack the bone well and season them
as before, & fill your pan as you think fitt with butter
and when it is baked do as above directed.

Venyson to keep a yeare

Take the haunch, boyle it a little, season it with 2 Nuttmeggs, a good quantity of pepper and salt, mingle them all together, and putt to it 2 spoonfull of white wine vinegar, then make the vennyson full of holes and putt it into a pott with the salted side downwards and lay 2 pound of butter over it and close your pott with some Course paste and lay a leatther upon the Vennison with a weight upon it to keep it down when it is cold. Spread the butter all over it thick, and a strong paper to keep the aire out, if the pott be narrow at the bottom, it will be the better, when you eat it you must turn it out upon a dish, with a plate upon it, and stick it with Bay Leaves, and serve it up with mustard and sugar.

7

Sweets, Biscuits, Cakes, and Bread

How to Candy Ringo Roots

Take the roots that are not too bigg and weigh them, and to a pound of roots allow one pound 2 ounces of double refined sugar, then take the roots and wipe them, then boyle them tender, the water boyling before you putt them in. Then peel them, then open them and take out the pith and take out the sprouts and as each is so done putt them in Spring water then take them and size them, and lye them. Take the aforesaid sugar and beat it in peeces. Take as much water as will dissolve half the given quantity of sugar and putt in on a Charcoale fire. If there be any frume take it off, then putt in the roots being well dryd and string on a thread, dipping first one side, and then the other, then putt in the remaynder of the suggar by degrees so let it then do leisurely over the fire till they come to a candy height then take that out and twiste them, and lay them upon a rack, and dry them.

How to Candy Angelicoe

Take Angellico roots that are very green and tender, then cutt them as long as you please, then take them and boyle them, the water just boyling. If there be any very small, lye them in small bundles. When they are tender take them and skin them, then as you putt the skin off, putt them into warme water, stifle them to green them, take them out and dry them in a Cloath, then weigh them, and to every pound of roots take a pound wanting 2 ounces of single refined sugar, then take the sugar, beate it, and clarifie it, when it is done so take the roots and lay them in a preserving pann, and poure the sugar among them, and keeping till they come to a candy height so you make them into what forme you please, as braiding or putting into knots, then lay them upon racks.

❧❀❧

How to Candy Oranges and Lemons

Take the fairest and choicest oranges you can gett rough skin if to be paired. Bermudas oranges are the best, The best lemons are the largest and palest skin except you pare the ryme then boyle them, the water boyling fresh. If you do few lemons then you may do them together, if you pare them they must be severall when they are very tender taking care they do not breake, then dry them in a Cloath, then take to each half dozen of oranges. Allow a pound of single refined sugar, to have them Lye in syrup, and be sure it be well clarified, before you make it a sirrup, and so let it lye 4 or 5 days in that syrup, then take them and wash the Clammyness of them, and lay them upon racks to dry them, then take the aforesaid sugar and clarify that, putt your oranges in a candying pott, then take the Syrup and throw uppon the oranges, then take to every halfe dozen of oranges a pound of sugar more being well clarrified putt to the Oranges and so sett them upon the fire boyling them to a Candy height, being carefull in Straining them and turning of them, then lay them in racks, putt them in boxes.

To yce Raw Fruit as Cherrys, Goosberrys, Currances

Take of your fairest of such fruit and wipe them clean from dust, take the whites of eggs and beate them very well. Dipp your fruit into the Eggs then into double refined sugar finely beaten and foarthed so lay them on a board either by a fire or in the sun.

To make Marchpane

Take a pound of Jordan Almonds and blanch them, putt them into water and wash them and dry them, out of that water take the weight of them in Loafe sugar, being beaten and foarthed, and perfume it with Amber Greese only, then take the Almonds and beat them with Rose Water to keep them from boyling, then put in your perfuming sugar, and keep beating till it is a perfect paste, then take it and roll it upon a sheet of paper, then lay it upon a sheet of wafer. Keep paper under it, the oven not being too hot. Make it as you please, when it is almost baked enough take whites of eggs well beated wth a rodd and putt in a quarter of a pound of refined sugar foarthed and perfumed, then take them out of the oven, and with a ffeather spread the said whites of eggs and sugar all over them and putt them in the oven again and let them stand there for a little then take them out.

How to make Naple Biskett both long and round

Take a pound of sugar beaten or fourthed through a Coarse sive, to that take 7 eggs, whites and yolks, then take to that 15 ounces of flower, being fourthed through a fine sive, and take the said eggs, beat them well with rods, then putt in the suggar still keeping beating, when they are well incorporated putt in the aforesaid flower still keeping beat till it is all in, and keep beating till the butter come from the very bottom, then take the panns being well payred, and fill the partitions equall, then as they goe in the oven scrape some sugar lightly upon them, then for the remaining batter, take coriander seeds and carraway seeds mixt and so strew on the said batter, then put in a little sack and a little more flower as they drop upon papers or putt into panns.

How to make Mackroons

Take a pound of Almonds, blanch them and as you blanch them putt them into Spring water, then dry them well, then take the weight of them in sugar being well beaten and foarthed, then beat y^r almonds.

As you beate them putt in a little Rosewater and when they are halfe beaten strew in your sugar by degrees, keep beating till all your sugar be in, you may perfume y^r sugar with amber Greese and musk before you putt it in, then take sheets of wafers and drop them on putting a sheet of paper under the wafers before you putt them in the oven scrape sugar on them, let not y^r oven be too hott.

How to make Puffos

Take a pound of Double refined sugar very well beaten and fourthed, and then perfume your sugar with a little muske, Ambergreese and civott. Take a little gumdragon well dissolved in Rosewater and put as much as will make the suggar into a paste, then Roll it into what shape you will, laying them on 2 or 3 papers for fear of Colloring and if you will have them collored with vermillion if blew take smelt, if green take japp green, if yellow saffron mixed with white and turn into what forme you please, lett your oven be not too hott. And grumblies are the same but adding a little flower or starch, and so collored, only not baked but dryed.

To make Starch Biskett

Take 11 ounces of starch fflower and 5 ounces of the finest flower and 7 eggs but two whites. Beate the Eggs with 7 spoonfulls of rose water, then take a pound of loafe sugar foarthed and beate in the flower and sugar very quick for two hours them putt them in your moulds being buttered and bake them in a temperat oven, and after you have drawn them lay them coole, and putt them in the oven again to harden them, the longer you keep them the better they are.

To make Bisquett in a Pann

Take a pound of flower and a pound of sugar, dry them both well before the fire, take 8 Eggs and but the white of two of them, beate them well with a whiske, then putt them in the sugar and flower, beate them very well together for 2 houres, then putt halfe an ounce of Carraway, and half an ounce of seeds, then put it all in the pann and let it stand in the oven for an houre & a halfe, the oven to be hot as for tartes.

To make the Carroway Cake

Take a quarter of a peck of fine flower, one pound of Carroway Confits, mingle them with your flower then take a pinte of milke and 8 eggs and 4 of the whites and one pound of fresh butter, halfe a pinte of ale yest, boyle your milk and putt your butter into your milke. When it is boyling hott beate your eggs with 2 or 3 Spoonfulls of Rose water and halfe a grain or a Grain of muske is little enough bruised with a knife with a little sugar and mixt w^t y^r flower, and mingle it well with a spoon, and do not knead it at all, it will be as thick as pudding stuffe. Then cover it with a warme

enough of sirrop you may make a
litle more sirrup and boyle it very thick

To make plum Cakes

take halfe a pound of flower, halfe a
pound of Currance, 5 Eggs 2 whites, but
halfe a pound of Loafe sugar Searched,
take the Eggs and beate them very well
then putt in the sugar and beate them
very well; then take the flower and
beate it with a litle salt, then slice
halfe a pound of butter very thinn
and mixt with your hand till it is
very well dissolved, then take your
Currance well pitted, washt and dryed
with your hand, putt them all in then
take your Currance and butter then putt
them not too full

Cloath, and lay a Cushon over it and let it stand by the fire halfe an houre to rise, then take paper and saw it like an hupe the Compass of your Cake, and saw a Bottom to it of paper and flower it all over, then take a little fflower, and strew it lightly over the cake, and make it come from the tray then putt it into the paper, heep and flatt it down smooth with your hand, and putt it into the oven to yce it, mingle some Rosewater and fine white suggar with the white of an egg and make it thick wth sugar, and when the Cake hath stood three quarters of an hour in the Oven take off the paper of the side of it, and with a ffeather yce the cake all over both top and sides, and sett it in the oven till it be dry and candyed then draw it.

To make plum Cakes

Take halfe a pound of fflower, halfe a pound of Currants, 5 Eggs 2 whites, Cutt halfe a pound of Loafe sugar foarthed, take the Eggs and beate them very well then putt in the sugar and beate them very well, then take the flower and beate it with a Litle salt, then slice halfe a pound of butter very thinn and mix't with your hand till it is very well dissolved, then take your Currants well pitted, washed and dryed with your hand, putt them all in then take your Currants and butter them, putt them not too full.

A good plain Cake

Take 4 quarts of fine flower & put thereto 4 ounces of Carway weeds, some nutmegs finely beaten and a little Ginger & a pound of sugar, stirr them well together, then take 2 pound of new butter, worke it very well in your flower, by breaking it therein in small bitts, and thin, as you can putt thereto a pinte of good ale barme, a pinte of cream, and the yolks of 12 Eggs, the whites of two being well beaten and so work it together with y^r hand lightly. It must not be stiffe nor much wrought. Sett it to heate before the fire for halfe an houre, let your oven be hott enough to scorch the paper, then putt y^r paste upon Cape paper well buttered and let it stand in the oven an houre or more.

To make good woodstreet Cakes

Take a quarter of a peck of flower winchester measure, Then take a pinte of barme, a pinte of Cream, a glass of sack, a little Rose water, 2 pound of butter, 2 Eggs, a quarter of a pound of Loafe sugar, some Candid orange and citron, then mix your barme, Sack and Rose water all together, putt your butter in Cold water, mix the barme with the Cream and other things. When you have putt all together mix them all very well upwards with both hands, then Let them rise before the fire, so make up in small Cakes and bake them in a pretty quick oven.

To make an Excellent Cake

Take 5 quarts of fine flower and one pint of the yeaste, one pinte of cream, two pounds and a half of sweet butter and warme your butter and cream together, then putt them and the yeasts into the flower, with the yolks of 22 eggs and 6 whites, then putt them in a quart of a pint of Damask Rose water, throw in one grain of muske hath been infused in 7 ounces of fine sugar, mingle all those together in the flower then take about one pinte of flower more, and shake it over your dough, and let it Lye before the fire to rise about one quarter of an houre then put in about 8 pounds of currants. Let them be washt overnight in a little warme water and well dryed then mould them up in your dough, then make up your Cake, and lay it upon 2 sheets of brown paper well buttered or in a hoope then let it stand in the oven, something more than an houre and a halfe, then let it stand till it be almost cold, and take one pound of loafe sugar beaten and straned through a Tiffony and halfe a pinte of Rose water well mingled in the white of two eggs, beate all those together very well and goo your cake over and then set again to the oven till it be dry.

A Christening Cake

Take half a dozen quarts of flower and 2 pounds of butter and the whites of 6 eggs, beate them and take a quantity of good ale Barme and some Cloves and mace, two pounds of pouder sugar, half a pint of Brandy, 5 pounds of currants and some sweetmeats, Mince them very small and so work them into your cake.

A Cheese Cake

Take 3 quarts of new milk from the cow and boyle it, then beate 18 eggs with half the whites, beate them very well with a little Cold milk and a little salt, when your milk boiles poure in your Eggs keeping it stirring till you see it turn to curds and whey, and then put it in a strainer and let the whey come from it and season the Curds with sugar, currants, cinnamon, rose water, a piece of sweet butter, some civot, some Jordan almonds blanched and broken. Mix all well together and when its cold putt it into your puffe paste.

Sugar Cakes Lady owens way

Take one pound of the best flower finely sifted and dryed, and take a pound of new butter unsalted and let it stand in a dish before the fire till it be half melted, then take 3 quarters of a pound of fine Loafe sugar well beaten and sifted, and strew it in y^r flower with a few Carraway seeds, then put in your butter and a spoonfull of Rose water and knead it upward, and when it is enough Roull it out with your rowling pinn and then cutt them with a glass in small cakes.

To make Puffe Cakes Lady owens way

Take 2 pound of fine flower finely dryd and one pound of ffresh butter new out of the Churn and lay your butter in bitts on your flower, then take the yolks of 5 Eggs and the whites of 3 well beaten, and put to it 6 spoonfulls of good barme 2 or 3 spoonfulls of Rose water, then knead it all together, kneading of it upward that it may not be heavy, then roule it up in little balls till it be cold, and then lay it out in what shapes you please, only remember to lay a few Raisins or Currans on the top and Scarr them with your knife and yce them with Rose water and sugar and sett them in an oven hott enough for Mainshotts but let them not stand too long in the oven, the same oven may serve for the former when these are drawn forth.

Sugar Cakes

Take 2 pound of butter, a pound and a halfe of sugar, mix them together, then putt into it the yolks of 2 eggs, a little mace, 3 spoonfulls of Cream, 3 spoonfulls of Rose water then put into it as much flower as will make it stiffe as paste, if you please you may put in Currans or Carraway seeds, bake them halfe an houre in a quick oven.

Almond Cakes

Take a pound of Almonds and Lay them in water till they will blanch, then blanch them into Rose Water and put in a pound of beaten sugar, and a quarter of a pound of flower, 4 yolks of Eggs beaten till they are enough, have plates buttered then Lay it on your plates in what fashion you will, Let them stand in the oven head down till they be halfe baked.

Loafe Ginger bread

Take a pound of flower a quarter of a pound of Treacle, quarter of a pound of brown sugar, quarter of an ounce of Ginger, a thimblefull of Turmerick, and as much Citron and Lemon pill as you think convenient, 4 yolks of Eggs, & so mix it together & if there be want of Liquour put in some water, at your leisure, it may stand 3 houres.

To make a saffron Cake

Take halfe a peck of flower, at least a quart of new milk, boyle it and melt and throw in halfe a pound of fresh butter, and a pound of sugar, add to it, five penny worth of saffron, dryed and poudered, halfe an ounce of Carraway seeds, stirr them well together, and knead them all up with a pinte of good ale yeast. Lay the dough by the fire 2 houres before you bake it.

Another Saffron Cake

Take a quarter of an ounce of Saffron or rather more, one quart of new milke, one pound and halfe of fresh butter, a pint of very good Ale yest, 8 quarts of flower and the yolks of 4 eggs well beaten, dry y^r saffron very well and rubb it to pouder, and steep it in Sack, first mix a pound of poudered sugar in the flower, then rubb the butter in the flower, then take the yest and mix it well, mix the saffron milk and eggs together, the milke being very hot.

A Saffron Cake

Take 5 quarts of finest flower well dryed, a quarter of an ounce of the best Saffron well dryed in y^r bosom and ground in a marble Mortar, and Layd to steep 24 hours in as much pure spring water as will cover it, and let the cup where it stands be close tyed or well covered up, then take a quart of new milke, and put to it a quarter of a pound of good fresh butter, and three quarters of Loaf Sugar finely beaten, stirr your milke over the fire till the butter be melted and the sugar dissolved then open your flower and throw in your Carraway seeds, Salt & Sprinkle over it your Saffron water, then poure in your milke, with the butter & Sugar having first strayned into your Saucepan or milke a pinte of the best ale barme. If it be bitter, poure on a little water and let it stand all night. After it is well kneaded let it stand and rise by the fire, then make it into little Manshotts, prick them, and lay them on a Small Holdloafe or papers, & so bake them.

To make French bread

Take 6 quarts of fflower, a pinte of the newest barme, with the third part water, 3 Eggs, halfe a pound of butter and a little salt, if the barme be light and froathy you may take the more of it, beate your eggs and make a hole in your flower, putt in your eggs, and barme and wett it with your milk, being made a little more than warme, make the dough not so stiff as for ordinary bread, put your butter in either before or after your milke, worke it very well and make it up either in little Cakes or Roules, make them very flatt. [...] Let them stand in your peet covered with a warme Cloath until it be very well risen then putt it in a quick oven, stopp it close and in halfe an houre you may draw, break those asunder that stick together, and put them in the oven again to harden the sides.

8

Pastries and Pies
Sweet and Savoury

Memorandum

What sort of pyes are to be seasoned with pepper and salt viz. Vennison, Mutton, Gibletts, Rabbetts, Neats Tongues baked whole, all sorts of wild fowle, all sorts of tame fowle (chickens excepted) all salt fish, fresh fish must be seasoned with pepper, salt, mace, cloves and currants. You may bake veale or lamb with pepper and salt if to be eaten cold, if hott you may putt fruit and a Caudle.

❦

To make Puffe Paste

Take a quantity of sweet Cream, and boyle it with some Mace and cinamon whole, but beaten, then have ready beatten eggs, with half the whites, and in the beating put some cold Cream and milk, and a little salt and Rose water and good slew of sugar, and if you please a grain of Amber in a tied ragg, when you have stirred it all together, strain it throw a hair sieve and then fill.

A Puffe Paste

Take 3 quarts of fine fflower and make a quart of it into paste with the whites of two Eggs and a little cold water, make it pretty stiffe, and work it very smooth, and Roull it out like a pye lidd, then spread your butter halfway, and toss a little flower over it and double it together and roll it over again and spread it as it was before and this do till you have spread a pound of butter, then roll it out, for whatsoever you have, make it in the Coole of the day.

Puffe paste for Tartes

Take a quart of flower and make it into paste with the whites of 4 eggs and a little cold water, work it smooth, Roll it out as thin as a pylid having wrought your butter well wth y^r hands. Spread it halfway on the paste, then cast a little flower over it and roll it out again then Spread it, this do till you have wrought in a pound and a halfe of butter and so use it.

Paste for all sorts of tartes

Take fine flower, putt it to the yolks of eggs, butter and sweet Cream, wett these wth your paste for all manner of tartes, harden them a little in the oven.

Puffe Paste for Pastyes

Take 12 quarts of flower, 3 pounds of butter, 8 eggs and as much cold water as will make it into paste, then roll it out small and pretty thin and spread it all over wth butter. Cast some flower over it and Roll it up, then Roll it out again 3 or 4 times and so use, to 4 quarts of flower 2 pounds of butter is a good Roll, but be sure your water boyle.

Puffe Paste for any Pastyes

Take 12 quarts of flower and make it into paste with 2 pounds of butter and 8 eggs and as much cold water as will make it into paste, then work it smooth, and rowle it out pretty thinn, and spread it all over with butter, then roll it up and putt it out again and spread it as before and this do till you have spread in four pound and a halfe of butter, then make your bottom of ordinary paste, and let this be for the top, and if you bake it in a pan you need no bottom crust. For ordinary paste for pyes you need only take for 6 quarts of flower, one pound of butter is enough, but be sure that your water boyle.

A white wine Caudle for any sweet Pye

Take a pint of white wine and sugar, put it over the fire all but a little to mix with Eggs, then beate the yolk of 3 eggs and put the wine to them that you left out, and when your wine boyles put in your eggs still beating them, stirring till you see it boyle. Then take it off the fire and sweeten and putt it into your pye.

To make a Hare pye

Take all the flesh off the bone and beate it with a Rolling pin, and season it with pepper and salt, then cutt Lards indifferent thick and Season them with a little pepper and salt and a little verjuice, so Lard your hare, and when that is done roule out your paste and lay on baccon in thin slyces. Then cut your hare in bitts as you think fitt and lay it on that, so lay more baccon thin sliced over that again, and put in a bay Loafe, and grate some nuttmegg over them with some butter, this is the way you may serve Turkey, Duck, Beefe or Mutton or the like.

To make a Hare Pye (2)

Take your hare, parboyle it, cutt all flesh in small pieces from the bones, then put in a Mortar and beat it well til it be like paste but before you beat it season it. You may either take Beef suet or the fat of Bacon as much of either as meate, some mace, cloves, pepper and salt, a handfull of sweet herbs small cut, then lay it in your pye and Cover it with sweet butter and bake it. This pye may be eaten with mustard and sugar.

To make a Rabbitt Pye

Take the hind parts of your Rabbits and skin them down the back and cutt it into 4 pieces. Take a neats tongue, boil it and peel it and putt it into bigg slyces, and season it with pepper and salt and nuttmegg, and lay it into your pye, put a good slew of butter on the top and so bake it and when it is baked fill it with clarifyed butter so serve it up when it is cold.

To make a Lamb Pye

Take your lamb and break the bones very well. Take out the skins and season it very well with good slew of butter underneath and above and turn over.

To make Lamb Pye

Take a quarter of lamb and cutt it into small stakes, a Nuttmegg and a little pepper and salt and a pound of currants all sort of sweet meats as lettice, fennell, succory, Ringo Roots, green chives, oringade and a cup of Lemonade, blanched Almonds and a few of the tops of sparrowgrass parboyled with a little Lettice parboyled and then put it in your pye, a lay of butter on the top and so close it, when your pye is baked make a caudle of white wine and sweet butter and poudered sugar and boyle it thick, put it into your pye and serve it up.

For a Buttela Pye

Take Lamb or some veale, slyce it thin and make some balls, take some ssassages, boyle some Eggs hard, take the yolks and do not break them, a few Large oysters and a little good Baccon sliced very thin and season your meat very well with mace, cloves, pepper and salt season together and so mix your meat and lay it into your pye, put butter, throw in Cloves and when it is baked boyle some butter and anchovies and fill it up and serve it up.

To make a Pye of Mutton & to look like beefe

Take a few quarters of your Reddish mutton, bone it and skin it, and get some sweet blood or Clarett wine and season it as you season Vennison and work the meat in the blood and the wine seasoning and let it lye 48 hours then make it up and bake it, and as it bakes put some Red wine and putt in some beefe just as in other pyes of vennison.

To make a Calves feet pye

Take 6 feet and boyle them tender, take out the bones and shred it very well and small with a pound and a half of beefe just seasoned with a spoonful of salt, a quarter of a pound of sugar, some Lemon, one pound of Currants, some Rose water, some candid Lemon or orange, mix all and putt it in your pye. When it comes out of the oven serve it in a white wine Caudle.

A Rare Beefe Pye

Take a Surloyne of Choice beefe, bone it and take out all the sinnews from it, and beate all the flesh with a rouling pin, then take 3 pound of the best beefe suett, mince it very small, a little time, winter savory, Marjoram, penny Royall, and a few Leeke blades minced, with the suett. Incorporat those together with some fresh sheeps blood. Season it pretty well with salt and grass pepper, putt the beefe in a convenient deep pan, the flesh being stuft with the ingrediants and the rest put about it, let it Lye in the pann all night and in the morning put it in the paste, or pye, and sett it in the oven, by 6 a clock, and draw it out at 12, cutt it open and poure into it 2 pourings of good warm gravy, shake it well in the pye and serve it up.

To make a Veale Pye

Take Loyn of veale and cutt it into small stakes, then take a nuttmegg and a little pepper and salt and mix them all together and season your veale and mix them all together, then take a pound of Raisins and a pound of currants and lay into your pye, a lay of meate and a lay of fruit and save the best of your fruit to lay on the top of your meat and sweetmeats if you please, some sweet butter and so serve up your Pye.

To Make a Neats tongue Pye

Take your neats tongues, Boyle and blanch them and slitt them in the middle and so lay them into your pye, put good slew of seasoning of pepper and salt and two or 3 cloves. Throw in a good slew of sweet butter, and so roast it.

To make Minct Pyes

Take a fresh Neats tongue and parboyle it, blanch it, then roll into small with 2 pounds of Beef suet. Season it with 2 pounds of Currants, one pound of Raisins, mace, Cloves, nuttmeg and Lemon of each a quarter of an ounce, half a pound of sugar, six pippins and a spoonful of salt, a little Rose water, half a pint of sack, some candid citron cutt small, mix all well together and fill your coffins.

To make a Chaldron Pye

Take your Chaldron and the weight of it in Beef suet mix it together with salt, mace and cloves to season with and sugar, Currents and Raisins and some rose water and so roast it.

To make an Umble Pye

Take your Umbles and parboyle them and mince them with double the weight of your Umbles in beefe suet, and mince them up very small and season them up as you do a Mince pye and fill and bake. When it comes out of the oven take a caudle of wine and sugar and Rose water and a quantity of fresh butter put in pye and serve it up.

To make a Chicken Pye

Take 6 small Chickens, bone them as for boyling, season them within and without with pepper, salt and nuttmeg, lay them in the pye with the breast upwards and on each breast lay the bottom of an Hartichock, some whole mace, some yolk of Eggs hardboyled, some Raisons, some Currants, a little Candid citron or Lemon Cover all with sweet butter when it comes out of the Oven, put in a white wine caudle to serve it.

A Chicken Pye

Take the Chickens and beate them flatt then season them with Nuttmegg, Mace and Sweet herbs, Barrberryes, Lemon pill minced small, some balls of forced meate and some fresh butter. When it is baked, putt in the juice of a lemon and a glass of sack.

To make an Egg pye

Take 12 eggs, boyle them hard, shred them small with one pound of Beef suet, season it with a teaspoon of salt, a quarter of a pound of sugar, one pound of Currants, some Rose water, some lemon peel, cinna-

To make a Curb Pye

Take a Surloyne of Beefe and bone it and wrap it in some sweet blood with a small quantity of Red wine or Claret and let it lye 24 howres, then take some sweet herbs and Mince them, some Cloves, Mace, pepper and salt, and season it well, and lay it into your Pye whole, and put good store of butter to it, and so close it, and when it is well baked, boyle some Anchoves togither and fill it up, and so serve it to the table

To make a Duck Pye

Take a duck, quarter him and season it very well with pepper and salt & Nuttmegg, Lay one halfe in the midst of your pye, and lay the quarters about the hole, put good store of butter & so close, & when it is baked fill it well up with Clarified butter and when it is cold serve it up.

mon and nuttmeg, mix all together, bake it. When it comes out of the oven putt in a white wine Caudle.

To make a Courb Pye

Take a surrloyne of Beefe and bone it and wrap it in some sweet blood with a small quantity of Red wine or clarrott and let it lye 24 hours, then take some sweet herbs and mince them, some Cloves, mace, pepper and salt and season it well, and lay it into your pye whole and putt good slew of butter to it and so fill it and when it is well baked boyle some Anchovies together and fill it up and so serve it to the table.

To make a Duck Pye

Take a duck, quarter him and season it very well with pepper and salt and nuttmegg and lay one half in the middle of your pye and lay the quarters about the hole. Put a good slew of butter & so cook and when it is baked fill it well up with Clarified butter and when it is Cold serve it up.

To make a Pidgeon Pye

Take your Pidgeons and break there Bones then take a good slew of seasoning and some nuttmegg and make some small balls and roll them up in the seasoning and putt them into the bodyes of every pidgeon. Then take your seasoning and throw this on top of the pidgeons with butter and when it comes out of the oven fill it well with butter.

A Pidgeon Pye

Take pidgeons, and season them with pepper and salt, with a few Cloves beaten, and put some butter into there bellys and make little balls of minct meat and mingle with them some thin collops of baccon, and if you will the bottoms of Hartechorks, with Grapes or Gooseberrys and a little verjuice.

For a Turkey pye

Take your Turkey and breack his bones very well according to the season of the year, take some poultry or some woodcocks and season them very well with pepper and salt and stick cloves on the breast of your turkey and putt some butter on the top and Close and when it is baked fill it well up with butter and serve it up.

To make a Goose Pye

Take a goose and break the bones thereof and a Couple of Rabbitts and stick cloves in the breast of your goose and season it very well and putt butter on the top and baste and bake it and fill it up well with butter.

A Wood Cock Pye

Take your woodcock, brake the breast bone and cutt off the head and leggs and season them well with pepper, salt & nuttmegg and cinamon. Fill your woodcock full of butter so lay them in your pye, with their breast downwards and put butter on the top and so stuff your pye and stick the bills of your woodcocks on the top of your pye before you bake, when you have baked fill it up with Clarified butter and so serve it up cold.

A ffriccasie Pye

Take some young Chickens and cutt off the leggs and wings, take the flesh off the breast of the Chickens, take some beefe suet and sweet herbs and mince them very well then grate a little stale bread to it, and break a Couple of eggs into it and take good slew of cloves, mace and nuttmegg, a little salt and work it all together and roll it into little balls, as bigg as a small nutt, toule some long, and take your leggs and wings and break them and cutt them in small pieces, and likewise do the like with the hind parts of your rabbits and take some Cloves, mace and nuttmegg and salt, and season your meat, take a small faggott of sweet herbs and putt it into your pye, and take your balls round and Long and Lay into your pye. Take some Lemon and slyce it thin and lay it up and down in your pye and so stuff. When it is baked take some strong broath and Gravie, and some butter. Boyle them thick together, then draw your pye, and pour out the liquor as well as you can out of your pye, then cutt off the lidd, and do not break it if you can help it, and take your faggott of herbs out of your pye, then put in your gravy with the other things, and shake your pye very well together, put on the lid and so serve it up.

To make an Eele Pye

Take your eels and cutt in short Lengths and take good slew of pepper and salt and season them and putt in the butter on the top and so close them. For a sweet eele pye you must take currants and putt it in with your Eels and so bake it and when it is baked add a cordiall, take sweet butter and suggar, and boyle them thick and putt in your pye, then scrape sugar on the top and so serve them up.

To make a Salmon Pye

Take your salmon, bone & grate him and slyce him thin, then take some Cloves and mace and pepper and salt and so season your fish and Currants and putt good slew of sweet butter on your fish and so bake it and when it is baked take some white wine and sweet butter and a little white sugar and boyle them together and put into your pye and so serve it up.

To make an Oyster Pye

Take a quantity of your largest oysters and a little pepper and good slew of cloves and mace. Season and fill and lay a good slew of sweet butter and so roast it and when your pye is baked take some white wine and sweet butter and boyle together and putt into your pye and serve it up.

To make a Pottatoe Pye

Take your Pottatoes and boyle them and peel them and some pippins and lay them amongst your potatoes. Then take a little pepper and salt and season them and take Currants and Raisins and put on top of your potatoes good slew of marrow and all sorts of sweet meats before named, and putt in Sweet butter and so on and bake them then take white wine, butter and sugar and boyle them together and so serve it up.

To make an Olive Pye

Take a leg of veale, cut it in thin slyces, season it with salt, pepper, cloves and mace, take some of your olives and shred them small with as much suett as meat and season it with sweet herbs and a hand full of Currants, two Eggs, and make it into a pasty and roll them in balls the bigness of a wallnutt, and lay in slyces in the bottom of your pye and the balls at top with some raisins and currants run all with sweet butter, when it comes out of the oven, put in a white wine Caudle.

A Skirrette Pye

Take the largest skirrets, scalle them and peele them and season them with Cinnamon and sugar, take good store of marrow and season it with salt and nuttmegg then Lay your marrow in the bottom of your pye then your skirrets with some Citron and Ringo Roots when it comes out of the oven putt with sack or white wine Caudle.

To make a Hartechoke Pye

Take your Hartechoaks and boyle them very well and take the bottoms of them and lay them into your pye and take a little pepper and salt and throw upon them a good slew of marrow and all sorts of sweet meats and sweet butter and so fill your pye, and take your caudle as before named and putt in after it is baked.

To make a plain Mutton Pasty

Take the mutton and bone it. Take out all the skins and bone and season it with pepper and salt and a little nuttmegg and lay it into cold butter coffin and so fill it and bake it and when it comes out of the oven eat it.

Puffe paste Tarts

Take some good pippins and paire them from the button and quarter them, take out the core, putt them into water and boyle them til they be very tender, and when they are well boyled drain them and putt some pouder sugar and beaten cinamon and and boyle them till they thicken very well, and fill and bake them.

A Mutton Pasty

Take a shoulder of mutton, bone and skin it and season it very well, and lay some beef just underneath & so oven.

A Lamb Py Pasty

Take your Lambs and break the bones very well, and take out all the skins and season it very well, with good slew of butter underneath and above, and so turn over.

A Vennyson Pasty

Take your vennyson and bone it and take out all the skins and season it very well & lay some beef underneath and above and so turn over.

9

Preserves, Syrups, Jams

To preserve Barberrys to keep all the yeare

Take the fairest Barberryes and stone them in bunches, then have ready fine Loafe sugar pounded and seasoned then lay a layer of sugar, then a layer of barberryes, so do till you have putt in what you please, only let your last lay be sugar, and they will keepe all the year with a delicate taste and collour.

To Preserve Cherryes

Take your Cherryes and weigh them over against your sugar, then stone your Cherryes and let your sugar be beaten and strewd into the pan, and set yr Cherrys in one by one, then take some other Cherrys and Squeez them, then take the juice and poure upon the sugar as much as will Collour the Sugar red, then sett them upon the fire, and boyle and straine them till they be done enough, then pott and store them.

Conserve of Currans

Take the Curans that the juice was taken from and strain it, then take the weight of it in sugar and boyle it, then put in your currans and boyle it til it be enough, then putt it in a pott and keep it in your store.

To preserve Green Pippins

Take your pippins and scald them till they be soft, then peele them, have hot water to put them in, and keep them close covered till they be green, but look that they do not boyle, and to one pound of pippins put one pinte of water, and a pound and a quarter of sugar, make the syrup and skim it, then put in your pippins and boyle them as fast as you can, and be sure that y^r pippins be kept scalding hott, and let not the water boyle, nor suffer them to be done too much. They must be done between St. James Tide and Bartholomew Tide.

How to Preserve Goosberrys

Take the fairest and largest Gooseberrys. First take them and stone them and putt them in spring water as you dry them, then putt them on a slow fire and so take them of and putt them on. This is to green them, then take them out and lay them on a Cloath and dry them, then take the weight of them in double refined sugar, beat it and foarth it. Take halfe of that sugar and so much water as will dissolve it, then putt in some of the Gooseberrys, and take some of the remayning sugar and lay upon the Gooseberrys, and so continue whilst all is in them. Let them boyle fast till they look cloase, then take the Gooseberrys out and putt them into glasses, then boyle that syrup whilst it is very thick and when it is very thick, if you find you have not enough of sirrop you may make a little more syrup and boyle it very thick.

To Conserve Roses

Gather your red Rosebuds in the heat of the day being a little open, for if they be too close the conserve will be bitter, then pluck and slip speedily and to every ounce of Roses put two ounces of sugar very finely beaten in a stone mortar with a wooden pestle. The sooner it is done the more vertue and better colour it will have. The sugar must be strained in still as it is a beating and when it is finall put it into a pott, but fill it not. It will worke for a month. When it is old you may put an ounce of sugar to every ounce of roses and coat it over again.

To Preserve Wardens or great Large Pears

Take a wine quart of fair water, a pound of sugar of like sorts. To each pound of sugar take a quart of water. When you have Clarifed your sugar, and made it very cleare, put in your wardens or peares being pared, and let them boyle very slowly, close and coverd till you see them of a good Collor and tender. Turn them allways to keep from spotting, when they are tender take them up, and let the syrup coole, and when its thoroughly cold put them up and keep them all the year.

To keep all sort of fruit the whole year

Take y^r large white goosberys at there full growth but not ripe with the Stoaks on. Put them in a Cource Steem or Narrow Mouth'd Crock with a handfull of Sea Sand at the bottom. Fill the crock with Goosbereys & Corke it Down Close, bury it Close up in mould in a house the same way with Corans, Strawberys, rasberrys & all sort of stonie fruit but they must be ripe first. Gather them in the heat of the Day & lett every fruit have his stoack.

Aples, Warden pears or winter Burgumys Must be put in a wooden Cask, get Saw Dust & Dry it well throw sume in the bottom of yr cask then a lay of fruit then a lay of Sawdust so on till you fill it, if you put 2 sort in one cask keep them from one another. Cover them with bords you may keep them in a room but take Care no hay or Straw come near them for it will cause them to rot.

Clove Gilly flower Sack

Take the flower and cutt off all the white & to a bottle of sack put a good spoonfull of flowers or more and stop it up close till it is deep enough you may keep the flowers dry.

To make Codlins Green

Take your best Codlin apples, put them over the fire in cold water with something to keep them under-water, when the skin doth swark peele them, then put them in the same water, and cover it very close. Let them stand over a slow fire till they be green.

To make Codlins Green (2)

Take the best Codling apples and put them into Cold water and be sure you keep them under water and when you see they begin to brake take them off and peele them and put them to the same water and cover them as close as you can, and let them stand over a slow fire till they are just ready to boyle, and put the same peelings of the apples into the same liquor and take them off & cover them and let them stand in the same liquor till they are Cold.

Lemon Cakes

Grate your Lemons and foarce some sugar. Put them together, and as much juice as will wett it, then heate it, and when it is just hott drop it with your spoon upon your plates about the biggness of a penny and so keep them for your use.

To make Lemon Butter

Take a quart of Cream and boyle, then take 3 yolks of Eggs and whites, beate them together and putt them into the Cream and boyle them again. Crush in as much Juice of Lemons as will turn it to Curds, then put up in a Cloath, and hang it up till the whey be gone out, then beat it with some thick Cream, and season it with sugar.

Pippin Cakes

Take your pippins and Codle them, then take the papp of it, and beat it well in a Mortar, then strain it, and take the weight of it, and as much water as will wett the sugar, boyle of it a little then putt in the pippins, and boyle it till it be very thick, then spread them upon glass or in Little dishes and store them.

Quince Cakes

Boyle your Quinces and strayn them in a Mortar. Take theire weight in sugar and boyle it till it comes to a Candy height then put in the Quince, and boyle it thick. Put it into glasses and store them.

Rasberry Cakes

Take Rasberryes and stew them in a Gally Pott. To a pinte of that juice put a pound of Loaf sugar, boyle your sugar to sugar again, then put in the syrup and sett it over the fire, but let it not boyle, when you think it enough put it in glasses and store them and when dry use them on cakes or for your use.

Cakes Violett, or any other floars

Take the violetts and cutt off the tops and take double refined sugar with as much water as will wett, boyle it to a high Candy that it come to almost sugar again put your fflowers into Coffins made of paper, and poure your Sugar hott upon them, let them stand and Coole, then store them, thus you may make cakes of any other flowers.

To make Violet Cakes or Cakes of any other fflowers

Take the violets and cutt off the tops then take double refined sugar with as much water as will wett it, boyle it to a high Candy, that it come to sugar almost again, put your flowers into Coffins made of paper, and poure your sugar hott upon them, then let them stand and coole and store them, thus you may make Cakes of any other flowers.

Or thus

Pick your flowers, stamp and strain them, boyle your sugar to a candy height, put your juice to it and boyle it thick, and then drop it upon papers or plates.

Another way of violet cakes

Pick the flowers, Stamp and Strain them, boyle your Sugar to a Candy height, putt your juice to it and boyle it thick and drop it on papers or plates.

To make Syrup of any Sorte of Herbes

The best way is to stamp the herbe and straine it, and sett the juice up for a slow fire in a clean bottle and let the frume arrive. When it is clean frumed and strained through a Jelly Bagg, put to every pinte of this juice 2 pound of very good pouder sugar, let it again over a slow fire till the foam refresh, then frume it. Clean off and put it into a dry bason, and when it is cold glass it up, if you let it boyle it will keep the better.

Syrup of Clove Gilly flowers

Infuse your flowers in Balme water, borage water, heate your water & poure it to them, a quart to 500 Cloves and to every pinte of infusion take a pound and a half or 2 pounds of sugar, just dissolve it over the fire till the syrip froath, then take it off the fire and when it is Cold bottle it. Some say the longer you leave your flowers in, steep the bottle. The same way make your syrup of poppies but infuse them in Lettuce water and put in with them a sprigg of sweet marjoram and a sprigg of Rosemary.

Syrup of Mullberryes

Take your Mullberryes and strayn them. Then put the juice into a glass and let it stand 2 or 3 days until it is cleare, then to every pound of juice take 2 pound of sugar, set it over the fire till it is melted, then poure it forth. When it is Cold, put through a strainer and after put it into your bottles and let it not stand in the thing you make it in.

To make sirup of orances and lemons

To every pinte of Juice put 2 pound of double refined sugar first pounded and foarthed. You must strain your juice threw a seive, and then putt them in an earthen vessel in a cold sellar for a forthnight and stirr them every day and then bottle it up and it will keep very well a yeare.

Syrup of oranges or lemons

Take sound fresh oranges and squeez the juice—into a silver tankard is best. Then to a pinte of juice take 2 pound of loafe sugar, put something on y^r tankard to keep it close, stirr it once a day till all the sugar be dissolved, then bottle it up for your use, and it will keep all the yeare.

Sirup of Pippins

Take a dozen of pippins and pare them, quarter them and boyle them in two quarts or more of running water until it be boyled to a paste, then take it up and strain it and take a pinte of the sirrup, a pound of sugar and boyle it to a syrrup and within 2 or 3 weekes of it standing neare where fire is it will be a jelly and cutt with a knife.

Sirrup of Violets the best way

Take 2 ounces of the flowers take 6 of water and 8 of sugar, put on your water till it boyle, then put it on your flowers and cover them, then with the back of y^r spoon squize out all the juice and strain it into the sugar, putt it on a moderat fire. When it is hott take it off again, still stirring it till it be scalding hott and take it off again, this do till it be ready by no means suffer it to boyle.

Cherry Marmaled

Take a pound of Cherryes, wipe & stone them, then put to them a pound of refined sugar, and boyle them together till it is pretty thick, putt them into Glasses and store them.

Jelly of Currans

Take the Juice of Currans and there weight in sugar and as much water as will wett the sugar, and boyle it to a Candy height, then put in your juice and boyle it to a Jelly and so strayn it into your Glasses.

Jelly of Pippins

Take a dozen of the best pippins, pare and slice them and quarter them, boyle them in a pinte and a halfe of fair water till they be very tender, then strain it, put to that liquor a pound of Loafe sugar finely beaten, and boyle it together on a quick fire, and keep it with frumeing. When it hath boyled a pretty while take a little out in a spoon, and if it jelly when cold it is enough, and then you may put into it a little juice of Lemon or Orange, stirring it together, but do not boyle it after, so keep it in glasses or potts as you please.

Jelly of Pippins (2)

Take a dozen of the best pippins, pare them and quarter them, boyle them in a pinte and a half of fair water, a pound of Loafe sugar finely beaten, and boyle it together on a quick fire and keep it frummy. When it has boyled a pretty while take a little out in a spoon and if it jelleyeing cold it is enough, then put into it a little juice of Lemon or orange stirring it together so you may putt it into glasses or potts as you please.

Marmalad of Lemons or Oranges

Take Lemons or oranges and boyle them with 6 pippins and so draw them through a strayner. Take so much sugar as the pulp doth weigh and boyle it as you do other marmalad and box it up.

Marmaled of Quinces without water

Take 2 large Quinces and Grate them but not too near the core, Let them remain in a porringer 4 houres, then boyle 2 Quinces till they are tender in faire water, then pare them, & cutt off the meat but not too neare the Cores. Take more than halfe the weight in sugar & strain the juice from the grated Quince, & put them altogether and boyle them on a quick fire and pott them.

Marmalad of Quinces

Pare the Quinces and grate them, strain them and take a pinte of the juice to a pound of sugar, then codle other Quinces. Stew them and putt halfe a pound of that Quince to them, and sugar, then sett it over a quick fire and let it boyle untill it Jellyes.

Another way to make Marmalad of Quinces

Boyle your Quinces very tender in water and mash them very small with a spoon in a dish, then take a pound of Quinces, a pound of sugar, take as much of the water they were boyled in as will melt the sugar, then put in your Quinces and boyle them together over a gentle fire till they paste, then put it into boxes and let it stand till they be cold and cover them up it will keep 2 years if it be well crafted.

To Make all sortes of Conforts

Take any flowers you please & when you have picked them dry them, weigh them and to there weight take twice the weight of white sugar loafe and pound them with putting in your sugar by degrees when they are pounded enough put up in potts for your use.

The Best Sorte of Harts Horn Jely

Take 6 ounces of hartshorn, put it to two quarts of water, put it in a silver tankard, or Earthen pot, Cover'd up close that no water may come in, let it simmer all night in a pot full of water over a slow fire, then boyle it up quick & when you find by the spoon you stir it with, that it sticks to your mouth by the water be much wasted, strain it out & put in a little more than half a pound of fine sugar, a little rose water, a blade of Mace, a Stick of Cinimon, the Juce of as many Lemons as will give it a good taste, with 2 grains of Ambergreece. Sett it over a slow fire. Do not let it boyle but when you find it to be very thike in your Mouth then put it softly into glasses & set it into a store & that will make it to Jely the better.

Pickles

To pickle Cucumbers

Take your Cucumbers and wipe them with a Coarse
Cloath very clean, then put them in rowes in an
earthen pott, between evry row of cucumbers a little
Dill, some ginger sliced, whole pepper and sliced
Nuttmeggs and a few Cloves, 6 is enough for a pott,
then take white wine vinegar and boyle it with some
salt and a bag of the same spice before mentioned,
and pour it boiling hott on your Cucumbers and stew
them up whole that no steam may possibly gett from
them. Keep them whole covered and boyle your
pickle once or twice a fortnight.

To Pickle Cucumbers (2)

Take the smallest of them, and clean them with a
Clean Cloath, then lay them into a pott with only
water and salt, lett them stand 9 or 10 dayes, then take
the pickle and poure it from them and make a pickle
of 3 quarts of water and 2 quarts of vinegar, two good
handfulls of salt and ounce of whole pepper, let them

boyle halfe an houre over the fire then poure it into the Cucumbers, and cover them and put your store of Dill and Bay leaves, then let them stand 3 weekes and look at them.If they be not green boyle the pickle again and poure in that and this do til you see them green, thus you may pickle the parsley, Samphire, and Broom buds.

To Pickle Cowcumbers (3)

Take the Smallest Cowcumbers fresh gathered. Wash them in Salt & Water then put in a black Crock & throw a spoonfull of salt over them. Take as much white wine Vinigar as you think will Cover them and boyle it, put it Boyling hot over the Cowcumbers and keep in the Steem, boyle the same vinigar for 4 Dayes together once Every Day, then throw the vinigar away & take fresh vinegar. Boyle it once put it in urn in half a doz^n grains of White peper as Many of Cloves half a spoonfull of Swt Oyl & Cover them up for y^r use.

To make olives of plumes

Take Black Plumes while they are Green, put them in Strong Salt & water 2 dayes, then take them out & put them in a ketle with half vinegar & half water, Green Cabidg Leavs under um & over them, put them on a slow fire. When they turn an olive green, take them out and when they are cold put um in a jar with as Much White wine Vinegar as will cover um. You must put in the vinigar raw without boyling.

Throw in ½ a pint of Sweet Oyl, & Cover them Close.
Keep them in a seller.

Desserts

To make Cheese Cakes

Take 3 pints of new milk, boyle it and when boyled putt in 12 Eggs with all their whites being well beaten. Keep stirring over the fire till it turns to Caudle then take it and strayne the whey from it in a hair sieve, season the Caudle with a little salt, some sugar, Currants, cinnamon, add a pound of sweet butter, two or three spoonfulls of Cream, a few Almonds beaten.

A Cheese Cake the best way

Take new milke from the cow, put rennitt into it, then get it warme, and when it is warme break it, and put the Curd into a Cloath and squeez it till there is no whey remayning, then have ready a pound of almonds finely beaten, then take your Curd, and beate it in a stone mortar with half a pound of fresh butter. Continue beating till there be no knobs seen, then mingle your Curds and Almonds together, then take the yolks of 12 eggs and putt them into your Curds and then take a pinte of Cream, and when it is boyled put in halfe a pounde of Naple Biskett ready grated till it be as thick as a pudding. Mingle all those together with a little Rose water, a little Nuttmegg and Mace beaten, make your Crust of the finest puffe paste and putt them into plats and so bake them, wch will be done in half an houre, but your oven must not be very hott.

An Excellent pann Cake
Take a pinte of Cream and halfe a pint of sacke, and the yolks of 18 eggs and halfe a pound of sugar. Season it with salt, beaten Cinnamon, nutmeg and mace. Beate all these together for a good space, then putt in as much flower as will make it thick as will run easily over the pan. Let y^r pann be hot and frye them with Clarified butter.

To make them Crisp

Take the same Ingredients only, put not sugar into the batter, put in 14 eggs, cast away the whites of 9, Let be as thinn as can run, fry them Crispe and strew sugar over them.

Cloutted Cream
Take a great quantity of scalded milk, put it into milk pans, let it stand 24 hours, then divide it wth a knife as it stands in the pans, then take it up with a

Scalded Creame

Take the nights Cream in the morning
not shreing nor breaking of it, put it on a
slow fire, when it is scalding hot take it off &
let it stand 2 houres, if you please you may
slyce a manchett, & toste it, dip it in sacke
first, season it and lay it on dishes.

Rose mary Cream

Take a quart of Cream, put in a good quan:
=tity of Rose mary flowers, boyle it on a
slow fire, when it is boyled to a good thickness
take it off & straine it & put suger in it,
and when it is cold as now ~~winter~~ mi shput
2 spoonfully of Runnet in the dish, and it
will cutt like Jelly,

To make Cream with Eggs

Boyle your Cream with Mace & Nuttmeg, when
it is boyled take it off, Let it stand till the milk
is warm, then put a litle runnet in it and let
it stand till it be cold.

skimmer, and lay it into dishes, and keep it 24 hours before you eat it, or longer if you will.

To make Frost & Snow Cream

Take some cream, make it something hotter than new milk from the Cow, sweeten it with sugar, Rose water, and put it in the bason you will serve it in, and put in a spoonfull of Rennutt, let it stand till cold, then poure on some white wine and sugar, whip some Cream and throw over it.

Scalded Creame

Take the nights Cream in the morning not stirring or breaking of it, put it on a slow fire, when it is scalding hot take it off & let it stand 2 hours. If you please you may slice a manshott & loose it, dip it in sack first, season it and lay it on dishes.

Rose mary Cream

Take a quart of Cream, put in a good quantity of Rosemary flowers, boyle it on a slow fire, when it is boyled to a good thickness take it off and strain it and put sugar in it and when it is cold as new milk toss 2 spoonfulls of Runnet in the dish and it will cutt Like jelly.

Goosberry Cream

Take y^r gooseberries & scald them then strayn them and mingle them wth Rose water then put your Cream with and let it be very thick.

To make Lemon Cream

Take a quart of Sweet Cream and boyle it well with Mace, then let it Coole, then take a Lemon and cutt it in thin Slices, and make it so sweet wth sugar that it may breake the Cream. Putt a little Orange flower water with the Lemon, then mix it with y^r Cream and let it stand till it be cold.

To make Cream with eggs

Boyle y^r Cream with Mace & Nuttmegg. When it is boyled take it off, let it stand till it be like to an eye, then put a like runnet in it and let it stand till it be cold.

To make Sett Custards

Take a quart of Cream or new milk, boyle it, in boyling put in a slice of cinnamon, a nuttmeg cut in thin slices, when boyled take it off the fire and beat to each quart of milk 8 eggs and to cream 6. Beat them wth half their whites and when pretty cold put in your Eggs keeping it stirring some Rose water and sugar, if you please a grain of Amber, and when you have put it all together strain it & put it in your Coffins being hardened in the oven and made with boyling water and flower.

To make an Orange fool
Take the juice of 6 oranges and 6 eggs and beat them, a pint of Cream, a quarter of a pound of sugar, and let it boyle till it is pretty thick then put in a little piece of butter and stir till it is cold then put in your dish.

To make Jelly
Take 4 calves feet or Knuckles of veale and boyle them very well, then poure out the water and put new clean water to them, and boyle it so long till you see them all jelly and when it is Cold strain off the fatt, and boyle it again with sugar, the juice of a lemon, some sack, whole mace and cinnamon, beate the whites of Eggs and putt into them, strain again throw a jelly bagg.

To make a Milk potage
Take your milke and set it over the fire a boyling with some sugar, then take as many whites of eggs as you think will serve, and whip them to a strong froath, then sett the dish that you design for the potage over the fire, and when it is hot lay the whites on the brime and settle it with a knife, then take a hot fire shovell,

and hold it over the whites to make them brown but have a care of melting your dishe. Then take french bread in slyces and put them in the dish and poure it over the breade and strew sugar over it.

To make a Sackposset

Take a quart of Cream or new milk, boyle it with some grated bread, then take 8 Eggs with halfe the whites, beate them well with a pint of sack, a half a pound of sugar, some Cinamon, mix them in the bason you will serve it in, sett it over some Charcoal fire till it begins to thicken, when pretty thick poure in your milk just boyling of the fire, stir it well, cover with a pewter dish, take it off the fire, serve it with sugar and cinamon thrown over.

To make a snow sack possett

Take 15 or 16 Egg whites and yolks beate severally, beat the whites in a large bowl with a whisk, put into them a little sack and sugar, whip it to a thick froath, then put into the bason you intend to make it in, a pint of sack made very sweet, let it be scalding hott, then putt the halfe of the froath to the sack, and have ready a pinte & a half of Cream & sweeten that, then putt in a Nuttmegg in Large slyces, and when it is ready to boyle up put in your yolks and take the Cream off the fire, then set it on again, when it is ready to boyle and a little thick take it off & take out the nuttmegg and holding it as high as you can, poure it into your sack stirring it all the while, then putt in the remaynder of the froath stirring that about, and Let it stand covered upon Embers for a quarter of an houre.

A Sack possett

Take a quart of sweet Cream and boyle it, a manshott grated, then take 20 eggs and beate them very well with halfe the whites, and a pinte of sack and half a pound of sugar, a nuttmegg grated and put in a skillett by itselfe, and stirr it over the fire till it begines to thicken, then poure in your Cream and Bread boyleing hott, stirr it well to mix them, then have the Beason you intend to serve it in over a chaffing dish of coales and poure it in and let it stand, halfe quarter of an hour, then cast cinamon and sugar over it and serve it up.

To make a Possett, Comfortable

Take a pottle of cream, boyle in it whole cinamon and 3 or 4 blades of Mace, take 8 yolks of Eggs and 8 of the whites, beate them very well, mingle them with a pinte of sack and three quarters of a pound of sugar, one Nuttmegg quartered, a little grated cinamon, sett those in your basin over the fire, and when its hott take the Cream boyling off the fire, poure it into the other as high as you can standing upon a stoole, then set it on a gentle fire covering it with a dish, and when

Paste for all sorts of Tarts

Take fine flower putt to it the yolk of Eggs, butter and sweet Cream, wett therto your paste for all manner of tarts, harden them a little in the oven

A Whete pott

Take a stale loaf of wheat bread slice it thin, then take a little marrow and lay in the bottom of the dish, then lay more slited bread and some Raisins and marrow till the dish be almost full then take Cream, Eggs & Nuttmeg & sugar and beate it altogether as you do a Custard then putt it in the dish and sett it in the oven, when it is baked you may put in a few dates in it the quantity of all is as you see fitt.

it good

it is well settled strew a little fine sugar on the top of it mingled with 3 grains of Ambergreese.

A White pott

Take a stale loafe of wheat bread, shred it thin, then take a little marrow and lay in the bottom of the dish, then lay more sliced bread and some Rasins and marrow till the dish be almost full. Then take Cream, Eggs, & Nuttmegg & sugar and beate it altogether as you do a Custard, then put it in the dish and set it in the oven, when it is baked you may eat it, stir a few dates in it the quantity of all is as you see fit.

A White Pott (2)

Take a pinte of Cream and a pinte of new milk, boyle it well wth Nuttmegg & Cinnamon, then take 8 yolks and 3 whites of Eggs well beaten, stirr it into the Cream, then take a manshott & cut it in broad pieces and lay it in a dish, then take marrow, Lay it in bitts upon the bread, and when the cream is cold poure it on the bread being sweetened wth it. Put it in the oven and bake it.

To make a whipt sillibub

Take the whites of 3 Eggs, some white sugar and Rhenish wine or sack and whip it in a Bowle wth a burch rod til it froath, then put in a quart of sweet creame and whip it in it. As the froath rises, skim it off with a spoon, and put it into your Glasses, and if you will have them cold, you must whip them in Clarett.

To make a Tansy

Take a manshott & grat it and take 20 Eggs with halfe the whites, and beate them well, with a pinte of Creame, three good handfulls of sugar, a Nuttmegg, some Cinamon, a little sack, beate your herbs and strain them, put your bread and halfe a spoonfull of salt, three spoonfulls of fflower, then mix them altogether and make it pretty light then make them up with a printe and bake them not too much.

A Tansy

Take Tansy, prim[rose?], Strawberry, select Suttony, or what hearbs you like, as much as will make it green, pound them and strayn them, breake 20 Eggs, take the yolks of all, but the whites of 7 or 8 of them, then Mingle your juice and Eggs, then take a couple of Manshotts grated and done threw a hair sieve, and put as much cream as will wett the bread Crums with some nuttmegg, Cloves, Mace, and Cinamon. Then put your juice to y^r bread and cream with a spoon full of wheat flour and a little sugar, so bake it with fresh butter, and stirr it till it be almost baked enough, and turn it once in your pan and when you have layd it in the dish or plate, sprinkle a little Rose water on it. Scrape on some sugar, and put some sweet butter and vinegar under it. Wheat blades, wallnutt Leaves, Alhoof, Spinage, any of these herbes will make a good tansy.

A Pudding

Take a pint of Cream and a Mannshott and boyle it together till it be thick, let it stand till it be cold, then beate 6 yolks and 2 whites of Eggs and putt nutmeg, sugar & rosewater in it, then tye it in a Cloath and boyle it for an houre.

Another Pudding

Take 2 or 3 french Rolls or white penny loaves. Cut them in thin slices and put to the bread as much Cream as will cover it, put it on the fire till the bread and cream be very warme, then take a Ladle and beat it very well together, put to this 12 eggs & but 4 whites, beefe suet or marrow according to your digestion, then put a pretty quantity of raisins & currans, season it wth a Nuttmegg, Mace, Salt and Sugar, put very little flavour for it will make it solid and heavy, make as much puffe paste as will make a rimm for the dish and cutt in whatever fashion you please, butter the bottom of your dish and sett it in a pretty quick oven.

A Baked Pudding

Take a pinte of good thick Cream, boyle it, when you take it of, putt it into half a pound of fresh butter, stirr it altogether till it be cold, take halfe a dozen Eggs, both yolks & whites, beate them together, and put into the Eggs a handfull of fine flower, and a handfull of white bread Crums, and stirr them altogether, with a little Cloves, Mace and Nuttmegg & Sugar. Take a Manshott and cutt it in round sippets and melt some butter, in the dish bottom to put under this, then bread, then lay the sippets then poure as much melted butter as will wett the bread, and when you intend to sett it in the oven, then take preserved Damsons or cherryes or both, then poure it on the sippets, and lay the round sippets in Cream on the topp of your pudding. If you have not damsons or cherryes, then strew on raisins of the sun stoned.

To make an Almond Pudding

Take a manshott and cutt off the crust and cutt the soft in thinn slyces, boyle a quart of cream, and when it boyles poure it all over your bread and cover it, and when it is soft bruise it with the back of a spoon and when it is bruised put in a quarter of a pound of jordan almonds blanched and beate 12 eggs with half the whites, some sugar, a little rose water and marrow if you have it, if not melt half a pound of butter and mix with it 4 spoonfuls of fine flower. This pudding you may either boyle or bake, but let it not boyle above halfe an houre and melt butter with salt and sugar, and poure all over it and serve it up.

Almond pudding wth french Rolls or naple Biskett

Take a quart of Cream, boyle it with whole spice, then take it from the fire and put in 3 naples biskett, or a penny French Roull, slyced thin and cover it up to scald it, when it is cold put in 4 almonds blanched and beaten wth Rose water, the yolks of 8 eggs and a little Marrow, with as much Sugar as you think fitt and a little salt. You may boyle it or bake it or putt it into skins, but whether it be boyled or baked, put sugar upon it when you serve it up.

A Carrott Pudding

Take a manshott, paire off the crust, slice it into as much milk as will cover it, let it have a boyle or two, then sweeten it to y^r taste with sugar and Nuttmegg, and take 12 eggs but 6 whites, 2 or 3 small carrotts grated, stir all those together, then take half a pound of fresh butter, well drawn, & poure it in stirring it well, you may put in a spoonfull or two of Rose water, then rub the bottom and sides of your dish with fresh butter and put paste about your dish.

To make a Green Pudding

Boyle a pinte of Cream, pare off the crust of a Manshott, then slice it thinn, put it in when the Cream is scalding hott and Cover it close till it is scalded. Mix them together and season it with salt, Cinamon & Nuttmegg, & put to it half as much flower as bread, some butter if you please, halfe a pound of Beefe Suett. Strain in it as much Spinnage as will green it, and putt marrow in great slices.

To make a Hartechoke pudding

Boyle a quart of Cream with whole spice, then put in halfe a pound of sweet Almonds blanched and beaten with Rose water, when these have boyled well take over from the fire and take out the spices and when it is almost cold, beate the yolks of ten Eggs, and as much sugar as you think fitt with a little salt, then beate the bottoms of six hartechokes and mix with your cream, and a pound of marrow, then putt it in a dish with puff paste and bake it but not too much.

Hedghogg Pudding

Take a 2nd loafe wett wth faire water & a little milke, 5 yolks & 3 whites of Eggs, grated Nuttmegg, Salt, Sugar, Rose Water and butter. Put those up close in a wooden dish bound with a Cloath, and put it into a seething pot, and when it is boyled stick it full of blanched Almonds or Raisins of the Sun, or dates sliced and cutt in Long peeces, and pore melted butter over it.

To make Oatmeal pudding

Take a quart of cream and boyle it. When it is boyled take oatmeal flower finely softened and stirr it into it wth the yolks of eggs spiced & sugar as you think fitt, then putt it into a dish and bake it till it be brown, you may put in marrow or suet as you please.

To make an Orange Pudding

Take the yolks of 14 eggs, beate them very well, then take a quarter of a pound of Oranges candied and cutt them small, as thin as you can, take halfe a pound of white sugar, and halfe a pound of sweet butter, melt it and beate all these together, then butter a dish and lay in the bottom some toaste thin broyled, then pour in your pudding and cover it with puffe paste and bake it, and let it not stand over three quarters of an houre in the oven.

To make a quaking pudding

Take a stale white Loafe, slice and put it into a quart of Cream, then take one Nutmeg, a blade of mace and a little Cinnamon and a quarter of a pound of Loafe sugar, six spoonfulls of flower, the yolks of 2 eggs, the whites of three well beaten. Mix all those very well together, then fflower y^r loafe well and boyle it an houre, and stick the top wth Almonds if you please.

Rice Pudding

Take halfe a pound of Rice, boyle it over night in a quart of Cream, then let it stand untill next morning to swell, then putt it out into a bowle. Mingle it with a quart of Creame the yolks of 12 Eggs and the whites

of 5, a pretty deale of grated bread, a little salt, a
pound of sugar, some Amber Greese, a little Nuttmegg & Mace, then put in of your best Beefe suet
shredd it very small, as much as will make them fatt,
then fill the Gutts and bake them.

A Very good Pudding

Cutt a mannshott into thick slyces & boyle it in
Cream or new milk till it be indifferent thick, then
take it up and put in 6 yolks and 3 whites of eggs,
season it with mace, Nuttmegg and Sugar, when they
are mixed well tye them up in a Cloath and boyle it,
sauce it with Rose Water, Butter and Sugar.

To make a puding to rost

Take a pint of Cream, scald a little grated bread in it,
then put in 3 Eggs beaten, a little flower, curans,
beaten Spice, Sugar & Salt with some Beef Suet
finely shred, make it prity Stife & wrap it in a lamb
Caul & rost it on a spit with a lyon of lamb. If you
pleas, you may put in a little Rose Water.

12

Drinks

A rare Secret for Sider

Lett your vessels be scalded 3 times over with hay
and Cow dung in boyling hott water. Just before you
put up your sider, smoake it with a taper of Brimston
and stop it up very close till you tann[?], then throw in
a sprigg of Clary wch you must seasonably gather, and
keep dry for that purpose, let not your sider stand in
a beer sellar, when you think fitt bottle it after the
usual manner, with a lump of sugar in each bottle, and
it will keep the yeare about and drink like Rhenish.

To make Almond Milke

Take barley and Boyle it in two or three waters, then
take halfe your Almonds blancht, beate them and put
them in a little Rose water, then Strain them into the
Barley water and sweeten it with sugar.

To make Cherry Wine

Take good cherryes, bruise them with your hand very small, so let them stand in a close vessel of stone, in a sellar or cold roome, then run them through a strainer and to every gallon of juice put 3 quarters of a pound of loafe sugar. Let it stand a day to cleare. You may put in some sack that will make it the stronger, to every bottle put halfe an ounce of sugar and tye it up close.

Couslip Wine

To each Gallon of water add 2 pound of fine sugar, 2 rootes of Ginger. Let these dissolve over a hott fire to boyle about halfe an houre and let it into severall earthen panns or the like to Coole and it being as cold as wort finally is, then let it a working with some pure ale yeast in this liquor. And for every 6 Gallons halfe a peck of couslips will be beaten in a mortar, but they must be in the Liquor while it is on worke and that by degrees it might worke the better, and when it hath mingled 4 or 5 hours, turn it up into a bason or vessel, in wch it having been 5 or 6 days bottle it up in good bottles. Press in your corkes a fifth and then tye them up.

Cowslip Wine (2)

Take 5 Gallons of running water, a baskett of Cowslips flowers picked, 2 pounds of mulligan Raisons washed and shredd. Put all into a good vessell, cover it with a clean linnon cloath, then a blanket. Let it stand in a roome where it have some aire to the fire 3 days, but stir it 3 times a day, for it will work the flowers. Strain it through a hair sieve and put it into a little Rennett, when it stood 3 or 4 days bottle it put into every bottle a lump of sugar and tye it down close.

Curran Wine

Take your currans & bruise them and let them stand that night, next day put 4 quarts of water to a pound of sugar and put it and your currans together and let it stand one day in the heat. Bottle it and put in some lumps of hard sugar and tye it very close with good Corke, you may keep it halfe a year. You may for small wine put more water upon the currans and let it stand as the other, but this will be ready to drink in a weake. You may make Rasbery wine the same way.

Goosberry wine

Take a peck of ripe Goosberrys, bruise them and put a quarte of spring water to them and let them stand 10 days. Then draw of the water and put a pound of sugar to 5 quarts of the water and let it stand one day to cleare. Then bottle it with some Lumps of hard sugar in every bottle and corke them very well and put it into a sellar. You may drink it at a month to five weeks old.

M*rs* Jones' of Adamstown goosbery wine

Take a cask of what size you please & fill it with pict goosberys then power to them as much cold water as will fill up the cask & let it stand for a month. Stop lose then draw it off & measure yr Liquor. Put to four quarts of liquour a quart of honey. Boyle it like Mead, when it is almost cold put Barme to it & when it has done working turn it in a cask that it will fill, stop it up and bottle it when you think fit.

Rasberry wine

Take to every quart of white wine 3 pints of rasps bruised and straned. To every quart of this Liqour put one quarter of a pound of sugar. Strain it and bottle it. You may use sack or Rhenish or white wine.

Rasberry Wine (2)

Take to a gallon of sack, Rhenish or white wine 3 quarts of Raspsberrys and halfe a pound of sugar, let it stand in a sellar 2 or 3 dayes, then strain it and let it stand one night to settle. Then bottle it very close and in every bottle put a lump or two of sugar.

Orange Water

Take a hundred of the best fruit oranges and pare all the Ryne from the orange skin, then take the peele and cutt it into small pieces and putt them in an earthen pott and putt 9 quarts of the best brandy to them and tye them up Close with a leather cover and let them stand so for 2 days and 2 nights. Some use to mix 2 or 3 quarts of faire spring water or sack to the brandy. Then distill them either in an Allembisk or Cold Still with a very slow fire. If you bruise the peel a little in a stone mortar before you putt them in the pott to keep it will be the better and stronger of the oranges. The first coming will be very strong, the second not so strong and so to the 3 and 4th will be the weaker by degrees, therefor to make your water more drinkable you may mix the severall degrees, as you think fit after this water is so distilled, you must mix into the water 3 or 4 pounds of the best refined sugar to quallifie the fiery heat of the liqour wch otherwise is not to be drunk.

Orange Water (2)
Take a gallon of Mallaga Sack, 20 good oranges, pare them so thin that no white appears, then putt them into the sack 24 hours, then still both together in a Glass Still, or in an Allembisk, and put sugar Candy into the glasses in which you reserve the water, keep the fruit by iself it is the best, you may do this with Lemons or Citrons.

Orange Water (3)
Take one hundred of oranges, 10 bottles of Rum, two bottles of Stale beer then paste up your still, keep a

constant fire and wett Cloaths to keep it Coole, you may deport from the rum 10 bottles of good water, poure them all out into an earthen store, and add thereinto a pound and a half of the best white pouder sugar. Stirr all well together, and paste the Steam up close again till that day fourth night then take it up cleare and bottle it.

The new orange water
Take one quart of fine brandy & put the cleare peel off 3 oranges, three quarter of double refined sugar & sixpennyworth of the best postalls finely beaten.

Rose Mary Water
Take 6 quarts of sack, one pound of cinamon grossly beaten, half a pound of flowers and tops of Rosemary, halfe a pound of Raisons of the sun, Stoned and Sliced, steep all these in the sack 12 houres, then still them through an Allembisk, put sugar candy finely beaten into the water.

PART II

13
Medicines and Cures

DISCLAIMER

The entries which follow were written in the 17th and 18th centuries. Medical science was not then what it is today, in the 21st century. Readers should not take what follows to be intended to give modern and/or effective recommendations of medical, psychological, or other advice regarding the treatment of particular illnesses. This part of this book is NOT intended to be a replacement for good medical diagnosis and treatment by a licensed physician or for care by a certified health-care practitioner. It is given only for historical interest as a description of "medicines and cures" recorded by the author over three centuries ago.

Some Receipts of Mr Boyle the Famous Chimist

For Coughs especially such as proceed from Rhumes

Take of Choice Olibanum finely beaten and poudered from one Scruple to half a dram, and mix carefully with it an equally weight of sugar Candy (white or brown) or, in want of that, of fine sugar, and let the patient take it at bed time in the pulp of an apple or some other propper. Add it amont for severall nights together. If it be found needful, it may be taken at any other time when your stomack is empty.

For Sharpness of Urine
Take of the dry stuff that divides the Lobbs of the kernels of Wallnutts. Beate them to a powder and of this give about halfe a dram at a time in a draught of white wine or possett drink made with or in any other convenient Liquor.

To appease the Violent pain of the Toothach
Make up a scruple of pillule, mash it and half a grain of laudanum in it two or three pills for the patient at bed time.

An Excellent drink for the Scurvy
Take two handfulls of Water Trefoil, let it work in about 8 Gallons of worte in stead of hopps, or of smale ale or worte made for it, and let the patient use it for all, or great part of, his ordinary drinking.

For the Yellow Jaundies
Take an ounce of Castle soap (the older the better), slice it thin, put it into a pinte of small beer cold, sett it over the fire, let it boyle gently halfe away. After

boyling some time straine it once, then strain it through a small sive, warme it, and drink it all in a morning fasting, take a small Lump of sugar after it, and fast two houres or three, the party may walk about his busyness and eat his accustomed meales, if at any time he drinke wine, let it be white wine if he be farr gone in the distemper 2 or 3 days after he may take it once or twice more and no oftener, refrain all other mornings. It will keep a week or Longer.

For the Jaundies

Take 2 or 3 ounces of Hempseeds and boyle them till the seeds (some of them) begin to burst, and a little longer in a sufficient quantity of new milke to make one good draught, which the patient is to warme, renewing it (if need be) for some days together.

For Convulsions Especially in Children

Take earthworms, wash them well in white wine to cleanse them, but so as they may not dye in the wine, then upon hollow tyles, or between them, dry the worms with a moderat heat and no farther than that they may be moderately or conveniently beaten to pouder to an ounce wth added pretty number of Grains of Ambergreese, both to perfume the powder (whose scent of itself is rank) and to make the modicum more efficacious. The dose is from one dram to a dram and a halfe in any convenient vehicle.

A safe and easy Medicin in Fitts of the stone

Take sack or in want of that wine, and by shaking or thorough mix with it as well as you can an equall quantity of Wallnutts oyle, and of this mixture give for 4 or 6 or 8 or 10 ounces at a time as a Glister.

For the Piles

Take the powder so prepared as in the former receipt (but leaving out the Ambergreese) and incorporat in exactly with as much Hens grease as will serve to make it up in an ointment. Apply that to the parte affected.

For the Piles (2)

Take Balsome of Sulpher made with oyle of tirpontine, oyntment of tobacco, equall parts thereof. Mix them well and annoint the greived place.

For Tumours or pains of the Hemorhoids not much inflamed

Let the patient dipp his finger in Balsome of Sulphur made without Turpentine, and with his finger so besmeared annoint the Tumors, whether externall or internall, once or twice a day.

To make Lime water
which is very useful in many Distempers

Take one pound of good quick lime and slack it in a Gallon of warme water and let it stand till all that will be settled at the bottom and (separation being made) the water seeming cleare at the top. It will often happen that a kind of thin scum and brittle substance almost like ice will cover the surface of the liquor. As soon as the water is thus impregnated delay not to poure it off warmly and keep it very well stopped for use.

A Lime water for obstructions and Consumptions

Take a Gallon of Lime water made as before and infuse in it cold sassafrass, Liquorish and Anniseeds, of each 4 ounces adding thereinto halfe a pound of choice Currans or the like quantitie of Sliced raisins of the sun, the dose of this Lime water is compounded in 4 or 5 ounces to be taken twice a day.

Amulet against Agues Especially Tertians

Take a handfull of Groundsell shred and cutt it small, put it into a papper bag of about 4 inches everyway pricking that side that is to be next the skin, full of large holes, and cover it with some Sarsnett or fine Linnin that nothing may fall out. Let the patient wear this on the top of his stomack renewing it 2 hours before every fitt.

For women in Labour to bring away the Child

Take about one dram of choice Mirch, and having reduced it to fine pouder let the patient take a draught of Rhenish wine, or sack or, if you would have the Liquor less active, white wine possett drink or any other temperate vehicle.

⊂⊱✥⊰⊃

For strengthening the Bowells

Take Cloves or Chives or Garlick and let the patient from time to time swallow one or two without Chewing.

⊂⊱✥⊰⊃

An Amulet against the Crampe

Take the root of Mojoaram & having reduced it to pouder, fill with this pouder, a litle square bagg or sackett of sarsnett or some sacks light stuffe which bagg is to be about 3 Inches square and to be hung by a string about the patients neck, so as to reach the pitt of the stomack and moderately touch the skin.

⊂⊱✥⊰⊃

For Staunching the Blood especially in wounds

Take those round mushrooms that in English are called puffballs when they are full ripe (wch is in Autumn) break them warily, save carefully the pouder that will fly up & the rest that remains in those cavities, and strew the pouder all over the parte affected, binding it on or proceeding further if need be.

For the dissentry and other sharpe ffluxes

Take the stalk, and leaves of the herb called ffleabame, dry it gently till it be reducible to pouder, of this pouder give about one dram at a time twice or thrice a day in any convenient vehicle, or els incorporat it into Conserve of red Roses.

To sweeten the blood and cure diverse distempers caused by accidity

Take Corrall the clearest and reddest you can get, reduce it (by grinding it on a porphory, or marble mortar to an impalpable pouder) this pouder give the patient of once or twice a day (as need requires), a large dose will ordinarily be about one dram at a time or from 2 scruples to 5. Let him long continue in the use of it.

For Convulsions of Children

Give the patient from 2:3 or 4 to 5:6 or 7 grains (according to the age) of the tonic, violet, oil, salt of Amber in any proper vehicle, it is not near so efficacious in full grown persons.

For Ulcers in the Breast and Elswhere

Take Millipedes (by some called Wood lice, by some called sowes) and haveing washed them clean with a little white wine and dryd them with a linon cloath beate them very well in a glass or in a marble mortar (for they ought not to be touched with anything of mettall) and give them first time as much juice as you can by strong expression obtain from 5 or 6 of them. This juice may be given in small ale or white wine, in wch the next time you may give as much as can be squeezed out of 8 or 9 of these millipedes, and so you may continue increasing the number that you employ 2 or 3 at a time till it amounts to 25 or 30, and if it need be to 40 or more for one taking, and note that if upon the pounding of these Insects you find the mass to dry, as it now and then happens, you may dilute it with a little white wine or some ale to be well agitated with it that being penetrated and softened with the Liquor, the mass in the better parte with its juice.

For takeing off the ffits of the Ague

Take good comon Brimstone and haveing reduced it into pouder or by passing through a very fine seive to the subtilest pouder you can give of this pouder one dram and a half or two drams made up into a Bolus with a little honey or els in any appropriate vehicle, let it be given at the usuall times, and reduced once or twice if need be, especially if the fits should return.

ffor the Pains of the Belly

Take of Myrhh, Olibanum & Comon ffranckincense of each a like quantity. Having poudered them, mix them very well, and let the patient receive the fume of this mixture cast upon a chaffing dish with embers in a close stoole, for about a quarter of an houer or more as he needs it or is able to beare it.

For a Cough Especially accompanyed with a tickling Rhume

Take equall partes of finely poudered olibanum and Venise Treacle. Incorporate them exactly, and of this mass forme pills of what largeness you please, of these let the patient take about half a dram at bedtime or if need be one scruple or more twice a day.

To prevent the Toothache or keep the teeth Clean & sound

Let the patient frequently rubb his tooth moderately with the ashes of Tobacco that remain in the pype after the rest of the body hath been consumed in smoke. Some time after (if need be) wash his mouth with faire water not too cold.

For the Heart burning

Take 15 or 20 to 30 or 40 grains of Crabs eyes reduced to very fine powder, and either take it alone or in any convenient conserve or syrup. It is for the most part best to take this medisin when the Stomack is empty.

For a Straine

Take the strongest wine vinegar you can gett, and boyle it in a Convenient quantity of wheat brann till you have brought it to the consistence of a poultis. Apply this as early as may be to the parte affected and renew it when it begins to be dry.

A Plaster to discusse Tumo^{rs}
or ripen them if it cannot discuss them

Take yellow wax ffrankinsence and Rosin of each 4 ounces or a sufficient quantity. Melt them together gently and being strained make up the mass for use in small rolls.

A Medicin for the Stone

Take the seed of fflixweed and give of it as much as will lye upon a shilling either whole or grossly bruised in any Convenient Vehicle.

For a straine

Take wormwood and pound it very well in a mortar of stone or glass. Then put to it as much of the whites of Eggs beaten to make as may serve to make it up into such a concoction as may be applied as a poultis to the part affected.

For a Loosness

Boyle a quantity of Corke in spring water till the liquor lifts strong thereof. Of this decoction let the patient drink a moderat draught from time to time till thus he himself finds him sufficiently relieved by it.

For obstructions and diverse diseases proceeding thence

Let the patient drink every morning fasting a moderat draught of his own urine newly made (and if it can conveniently be) while it is yet warme forbearing food for an hour or two after it.

For the Black Jaundies

Take a spoonfull of honey, boyle it gently and simmer it till it come to a good consistance, then add of wheat flower, saffron (reduced to a pouder) as much of each as you may take upon the point of a knife, and having mixed all well, put it over the Coals again til it loose its smell. Afterwards you may putt it into a little stone or earth pott and keep it for your use, which is the patient. Take the quantity of food and annount the navvell and fill the cavity thereof with it repeating the operation for some days together when the stomack is empty and abstain from meat and drink about 2 hours after the medicin.

An Easy Medicin for a
Fresh straine

Make up the Clay with wch the Bungs
of Barrells are wont to be stopped, wth
as much vinegar as will bring it to
the Consistence of an indifferently Ca=
=taplasme, then warme it a litle and
apply it to the parte affected

A Remedy much used
for Chilblines

Take a turnip roast it well under the
Embers, and beate it to a poultis then
apply it very hott to the parte affected
and keep it on (if need be) for 3 or 4
Dayes in that time shifting it twise or
thrise if occasion require it.

For Fitts of the Mother

Take and dissolve some salt in the best wine vinegar, and in this dipp a soft linnon Cloath, which being folded up as to make 3 or 4 doubles is to be applyed from what warme in the folds of the patients foot and kept till the fitts be over.

A good drink to be used in Feavers especially continued ones

Give into half a pinte of some small carbement[?] drink half an ounce of harts horne burned to great whiteness, which is to be boyled in the liquor and this thus altered is to be given from time to time.

An Easy Medicin for a Fresh straine

Make up the Clay with wch the Bungs of Barrells are wont to be stopped, wth as much vinegar as will bring it to the consistence of an indifferent cataplasme, then warme it a bit and apply it to the parte affected.

A Remedy much used for Chilblines

Take a turnip, roast it well under the Embers, and beate it to a poultis then apply it very hott to the parte affected and keep it on (if need be) for 3 or 4 days in that time shifting it twice or thrice if occasion requires it.

For the Collick and diverse other distempers

Take 4 or 5 balls of fresh stone horse dung and let them steep for about a quarter of an hour (or less) in a pinte of white wine, in a vessell well stopped that the liquor may be richly impregnated with the most volatile and subtile parts of the dung. Strain this and give of it from a quarter to half a pinte or some ounces more at a time, the patient having a care not to take cold after it.

An Easy Medicin to Cleanse the wombe especially after Child bearing

Take a large white Onyan of about four ounces in weight if you can gett so bigg a one, and boyle it in about a pint of water with any thing fitt to make a very thin broath till a third or more of this broath be consumed. Of this broath which may be made a little pallatable with nuttmegg or the patient is to take 6 or 8 ounces twice or thrice a day.

A good medicine for a sore throat

Take the white of a new layd egg. By beating thereof reduce it into water and with this water mix diligently as much conserves of red Roses as will reduce it to a soft mass, whereof the patient is to let a little bitt at a time most carefully into the throat.

To Make an easy Duretick

Peel off the Inner skin of an eggshell then beat the shell in a very fine pouder give about a scrape of it at a time in any convenient vehicle.

A Choice Remedy for a sore throat

Take honsleeke and having lightly beaten it in a glass or stone mortar press out the juice. Put almost an equally quantity of virgin honey, mix them well, and add to the mixture a little burned allom as much as will give it and your noble aliments together, let the patient take this from time to time with a liqourish stick or some fresh thing.

To make a Very good Sirup for thin Rhumes

Dryed roses the syrup thereof, syrup of Jobbs and syrup of Corne poppys, of each a like quantity, mix and use them as the nesesity of the sick require.

For the dissentery & Plurisie

Take and grate to a fine pouder the dryed pizzle of a stagg, of it as much as will lye upon a shilling or thereabouts once or twice a day in any convenient vehicle.

For a Hoarseness upon a Cold

Take 3 ounces of Hysop water. Sweeten it with sugar Candy, then beate well into the yolk of one egg and drink it at a draught.

✿

A Choice Medicin for the Jaundies in Children

Take half an ounce of Choice Rubarb made into pouder, incorporat with it by long beating two handfuls of well-chosen cleansed currants. Of this Electuary let the patient take every morning about the quantity of a nuttmegg for several mornings together.

✿

An Experienced Medicin
for strengthening a Weak sight

Take of Eyebright, sweet fennell seeds and fine sugar all reduced to pouder of each an ounce, Nutmegg also pulverized one dram (at night). Mix very well together and take of the composition from a dram to 2 or more from time to time.

✿

Another Medicin for Tertian Agues

Take cured allom and Nuttmegg fully beaten or rather scraped for each about half a dram. Mix the pouders well together, and with about 6 drams saffron give this 2 or 3 spoonfuls of white wine vinegar at the usuall time.

For Stuffing of the Lungs and the Chin Cough

Make syrup of penny Royall or of groundsell moderately tarte wth oyle of vitrioll, and of this let the patient take very loasly about a quarter of a spoonfull from time to time.

༒

For the falling sickness in Children

Take half a dram of chosen Amber finely poudered and give for 6 or 7 weeks together once a day when the stomack is empty in about 4 ounces of good white wine.

༒

An approved Medicin to drive away the Stone and Cure suppression of Urine proceeding from it

Take the roots of wilde Garlick (by some called Crow Garlick). Wipe them very well and stampe them very well in a mortar of stone or Glass, and straine out the juice, with which make a moderate draught of good wine considerably strong, and let the patient take it once or twice a day.

༒

An Experienced Medicin for sore throats

Take of Scabious water, 6 ounces of wine vinegar, a small spoonfull of mustard seed beaten and of honey each a spoonfull, stir and shake them very well together, then filter the mixture and keep it for your use.

An Easy but approved Medicin for the Chollick

Take about half a dram of mastik and mix it with the yolk of a new laid Egg and give it the patient once or twice a day.

To Appease the heat of ffeavers
by an Externall Remedy

Apply to the soles of the feet a mixture of thin cataplasme made of the leaves of the best tobacco fitt to be cutt to fill a pye with. Break up as much of the freshest Currant you can gett, as will bring the tobacco to the confusion of a poultis.

A Choice medicin for a Whitloe

Take shell snailes and beate them the pulp parts of them very well, wth a convenient quantity of fine Chopt parsley which is to be applyed warme to the affected parts and shifted two or three times a day.

An Excellent Remedy for a fresh Straine

Take 4 ounces of bean flower, two ounces of wine vinegar, of these make a cataplasme to be applyed while warmed to the parts affected.

For a Burne
Mingle Lime water with Linseed oyle by beating them together with a spoon and with a feather dress the burne several times a day.

For a Fresh Straine
Boyle Brawn in wine vinegar to the consistencie of a poultis apply it warm, and renew the poultis once in 12 hours for 2 or 3 times.

An Experienced Medicin for the Collick
Take of good Nitre an ounce, and rub it well in a clean mortar of glass or stone then grind with it halfe a scruple or more of fine saffron and of this mixture give about half a dram for a dose in 3 or 4 ounces of cold Spring water.

For heate about the Orifice of the Stomach
Make a syrup with the juice of Honeysuckle and sugar and give about one spoonfull of it from time to time.

To strengthen the stomach
& help the want of Appetite

Take the roots of Gentian (sound and not sapon-
nated). Pulverise with no more waste of there
moisture than is necessary. Reduce these to pouder, of
which let the patient take from 12 to 15 grams double
that quantity (or more if need be) twice or thrice a
day. It may be taken on an empty stomack, or if that
be not to conveniently done at meal times to correct
the bitterness, one may add to it powdered sugar, or
make it up use some fitt conserve or mix it with a
syrup. It is very good not only for want of appetite,
but for obstruction. And JRB have usefully given it
for vertiginous affectations of the brain and to loosen
if not quite take away the fitts of an Ague, and even
quartans, but in this last take the dose must be
considerably augmented one may use if they please
instead of the powder give the extract drawn with
faire water, and for those that like this forme made up
into pills with a sufficient quantity of poudered
turmeric or the like proper addicement to which I
have added sometimes some graines of salt wormwood, wth good succorr in fluxe that proceed from
conditions and indigestion, where the winter season
or the patients consitution imbibe or the modicum is
to be long kept I choose rather to make the extract
with wine moderately strong rather than water.

A Stomachicall Tincture

Take agrimony 2 drams small, and a dram of Coriander seeds burned and a scruple of sassafass shavings

and barke one dram, of gentian roots half a dram, of zeodory root 10 Grains, pour upon this the quarter of a pinte of boyling Spring water, cover it, and let it steep 12 hours then strain it and put it in a bottle then drop a drop of the oyle of Cinamon upon a lump of sugar and put into the Liquor. The dose is 3 spoonfulls twice a day an hour or two before meals.

For Fluxes Especially accompanyed with Grippings
Take a Lapis Callamintus finely poudered, two Scruples, of white chalk one scruple, mix them exactly and give them in a spoonfull or two of new milk twice, or if it be urgent thrice a day.

An often Experienced Medicin for the Collick Especially produced by Sharpe humo^{rs}
Take a quart of Clarett and put into the vessell about 2 ounces of nettleseeds, stopp the bottle and keep it in boyling water till the water has made 3 or 4 boilings to assist the wines Impregnation with the finer parts of the seeds, of the liqour let the patient take a small draught once or twice a day.

To make the white stone
Take one pound of saltpeter and have ready a Crucible, which is a goldsmiths refining pott sett into a charcoal fire, the Coales lyeing round about the top

of your pott, when you see the pott red hott all over put in the salt peter and let it melt, and when it gives over sling into it a small piece of allomm bruised in the cryings of a small nuttmegg. When that is done boyling throw in as much brimstone, and let it flame until it gives over itselfe then take the pott off the fire wth the tong, put it softly on the warme hearth a very little while haveing in readying about a dozen of silver spoons. When ready pour your liquour out as far as it will hang about the pott, lett it continue in your spoons till it be a substance, then take them out and lay them to coole in a window and when cold keep them in a box for your use.

It sooth bloodshot eyes a little of the powder being scraped and blowne into the eye through a quill, the same way used it sootheth a pin or webb in the eye, it sometimes sootheth the toothace a little bitt in the mouth and you may suffer anyone to swallow it, for it is excellent for sore mouth or throat, and good to promote a sweet breathe, and washe your mouth every morning wth a little or rubb your tooth, it helps to keep them from rotting.

In a feaver it allays the draught, it will help to cutt every phlegm, it will kill pimples in the face, or hand, being rubbed with fasting spittle often, too have several times cured a whitlow which hath been fixed long as 16 years another 10 years and several ulcers and ring wormes, only rubbing it on the sore with fasting spittle and eating some of it every morning, that is, bite a small piece and let it melt and swallow that down.

It once cured a violent canker in a Gentlewomans mouth. She wett the stone often in vinegar and rubbed the mouth with it. But it will smarte much the first or second time but after that not much, and when a sore mouth meets with this as a cure they must not use it often in the day and swallow it often also.

For soreness in the Eyes
Take honey and Carduns water, dissolve it together, heat it thoroughly upon the fire, if any frume arise take it off and drop 3 drops of a lime and cold at a dropping, this do 3 times a day.

For the Goute and Sciatica
Take halfe a pinte of sallott oyle, three ounces of Bees wax, two ounces of pounders white load, one ounce of white bean of ffranckinsense, mix all these well together and put them in a skillett, and let them boyle till it turns to a white froath, then take it off and let it stand for a little while, put it on again, and let it boyle to a dark Russett froath. Then take it off and let it stand for the spare of an hour then putt it on again and let it boyle till it be as black as jett then take it up and coole and when Cold roll it up with sallott oyle or white wine when you use it spread it upon new Bandle Cloath it will be 3 or 4 hours in doing.

Oyle of Lillies

Take of the white Leaves of Lillys
as much as you please put into a pott
and poure upon it as much as much of
sallett oyle till all the Lillies be well
covered, and then sett it the space of 14
dayes in the Sun or some other warme
place, afterwards Let them sieth in a
narrow pott in seething water, then
pull out the Leaves and put in fresh
againe, and then wring it out well,
do this three times one after another, &
then keep it.

Some approve of cutting away
the yellow, and to make ~~an two~~ in=
=fusions as the better way

Oyle of Lillies

Take of the white Leaves of Lillys as much as you please put into a pott and poure as much of sallott oyle till all the lillies be well Covered and then lett it the space of 14 days in the sun or some other warm place, afterwards let them sit in a narrow pott in seething water, then putt out the leaves and putt in fresh again, and then wring out well, do this three times one after another then keep it. Some approve of cutting away the yellow, and to make infusions as the better way.

Water of Wallnutts
called the water of Life for its vertues

First take wallnutts in the beginning of June. Break them in a mortar. Afterwards still them in an ordinary still. Keep the water by itself then take other wall-nutts and gather them about Midsummer. Use them as you did the first, take wallnutts the third time a fourthnight after Midsummer and so likewise to them keeping it by itselfe.

The Vertues thereof

First, it will heale all manner of dropsyes and parlysis drunk with wine fasting. 2ly, it is good for the eyes dropping and dropp thereof in them. 4ly, it will make ones face faire fit so washed therewith. Fifthly, it is good for all infirmitys within the body and driveth out all Consumption if it be so drunk with wine moder-ately or with water. 6ly, it will kill wormes in the body either drunk with wine or by itself. Who ever as such to drink much of it shall live as long as nature can possibly continue in them. Finally, if you have any wine that hath been changed put a little wine thereof and stop the bottle very well and within 4 days it shall be fit again.

Eye Water

Take Eyebright water one pint, white copper 2 drams, of alloe 3 drams, of white sugar Candy an half an ounce dissolve them all in a glass. Lett into a kettle of warm water. Beate your alloes finally or els it will not dissolve, a dropp of this dropped into your eye helps rhumes or blood or soreness in the eyes.

For the Morphen

Take the milk of an Ass mingle it with Lye, bean flower and annoynt the place with it and it will clean take away any spott or freckle.

Surfeit Water

Take the quantity of one handfull of mint, and one handfull of wormwood, take 2 handfulls of Carduus. Strip them from the coarse stalks that doth not break easily, and put them in the milke, then lay them in steep in new milk warme from the cow, just as much as will cover them pressing them down with your hand, and so let them lye 12 houres in steep between 2 earthen pans. Then put them into a Cold still with a quick fire, if your still be to hott put a wett Cloath upon it, when your still runs you must keep a slow fire just enough to keep it goeing.

Aqua Mirabilis

Take Gallingall, Cloavs, Quibibs, Ginger, Cardmom, Mace, Nuttmegg, and Mellilott of each a dram, the juice of Sellondine, in halfe a pinte of Aqua Vite. Mix them altogether, your spice being beaten or bruised, then stirr them alltogether your spice being beaten or bruised, then put to them 3 pintes of the best white wine. Stirr them altogether, and so let it stand all night, and then distill it in a glass Limbeck with a temperat fire.

Another of Aqua Mirabilis

Take 3 pints of sack, one pint of Angelico water strong, one quarte of the juice of Sellondine or water if the other cannot be gotten, of Cowslip, Mellilot flowers, Mayflowers and Cinamon of each 2 drams Nuttmegg, Ginger, Cloves, Quibibs, Cardamom and Galligall of each one dram halfe a pound, one pennyworth of saffron, of the juice of mint and juice of Barme of each half a pound. Bruise all these and mix all together in a cold still, lod it up with cold paste and let the fire be slack, draw it leisurely, the longer it is a-drawing, the better, dulcify it with double refined sugar, tye up two grams of Ambergreese in a little tiffony and let it hang in your bottle, poureing your water in one sponnfull is enough to take at a time.

The virtues of this water are many. It dissolves the swelling of the liver, it comforts it being wounded, it suffers not the blood to putrifie. It is good against the heart burning, it suffers not phlegme and Melanncholly to prevaile above nature, it expelleth the Rhumes, and promotes a good collour. It strengthens the memory and destroyeth ulcers in the Lungs, this being given at the point of death preserves them in death. The doze is a spoonfull once a weeke in the sumer and two in the winter of the strong, of the week that useth this water need not be lett blood, let all the dry things steep 12 hourse before you still them.

Jelly of Harteshorne

Take almost a quart of Spring water and halfe a pint of white wine and 2 ounces of Hartshorne 2 good spoonfulls of sugar. Stir all together and put them into a deep pewter dish upon a Chaffing dish of Charcoale, and cover it close, let it only zimper not boyle fast one houre and a halfe then let it out through a strainer, and put into it the juice of a lemon and put it into your glasses.

The hartshorne that is left at once useing may be put in again next time with more fresh harts horne and then you may make the more of it. This is good for sick or weak folks, to whom you may also make some good broath of a knuckle of veale and put in it some harts horn, a blade of mace and a crust of bread, and let it stand for two or three houre and then it will be the stronger.

For Shortness of breath

Take the lungs of a ffox as soon as they come out of the ffox, wash them in faire water from all the blood, then lay them in white wine vinegar all the night. Take them out and dry them in an oven. Beate them to a pouder, then mingle the pouder of ffox lungs with the pouder of Liqourish, Anniseeds, ffennel seeds and Caraway seeds of all the like quantity. Let your pouder be foarced well, and mingle them with so much sugar Candy as may make them fitt for your taste. You may take this pouder in the morning fasting, dry or in what you please, and at any time of the day as often as you can.

Another for shortness of the breath

Take the ffox lungs new from the ffox and lay them in hysop water 24 hours shifting the water twice, then wash them in Rose water and put them in a stone mortar, then have halfe a pound of sugar ready. Take some of the Lumps of the sugar, and put into the mortar, then beate them well together till all the Lungs be in a mash, then put in a quarter of a pinte of Hysop water, stirring them well together, then strain them into a silver skillett, and put in the rest of the sugar, then boyle them till they mingle together, and becoms like a thick sirup. Then take it off and eat it wth a Liquorish stick when you please.

§§§

For oppening obstructions of the Liver
& Spleen and for the Consumption

Take of Harteshorne strained, Agrimony, Liverwort, Vineleaves, Strawberry leaves, maiden haire, Colts-foot leaves, pollipodium, of each a handful, fine paresly roots and one ffennell root pilt and scraped, fine barely boiled in 3 waters, anniseed bruised, Liquorish scraped and shred, of each an ounce, Raisons of the sun, figs, prunes, of each a quarter of a pound stoned with 9 dates, boyle all these together in 4 quarts of running water in a pott close and covered or stopt upon a soft fire untill halfe be consumed, so strain it and sweeten it with brown sugar candy, and of this drink quarter of pinte in the morning, as much in the evening and it will quickly work a strange cure.

§§§

To Make Juice of Liqourish Cakes
wch Queen Elizabeth used alwayes for a Cold

Take one pound of English Liquorish the greatest and thickest, scrape the Ryme, clean off it, cutt them into small pieces and put them into a little pipkin with a pinte of Hysop water, cover the pipkin close, and lett it on hott Embers to infuse (but not boyle) all night. In the morning scrape the Liqour out and stampe the Liquorish in a clean mortar to gett all the vertue out of it, then strayne them very hard into a clean dish and sett the dish on a fire on a Chaffing dish of coales stirring it continually to prevent sticking on the sides of the dish. Let it waste and evaporat away but not boyle til it come to a jelly. Then, having ready a pound of double refined sugar with 8 grains of muske or Ambergreese beaten amongst it very small and sifted through tiffony, then take part sugar and part jelly and work them with musk. Labour in a mortar to a paste, and so by degrees worke the paste into what fashioned cakes you please or like best, keep them in boxes in allesect[?] or store near the fire till they be thorough dry, when you take a little bitt of the cake, lett it dissolve leisurely in your mouth and by doing so you will soon abate the vigour of the great cold. PROBATUM This was the Queens own cake by which shee found such good, that it is said shee had allways some of them about with her.

Snaile Water

Take a peck of Garden Snailes, and wash them shells and all very well in faire water, then dry them in a Clean Cloath, then breake them in a stone mortar and putt them asteeping in a Gallon of the best strong ale adding to it 6 ounces of hartshorn scraped into pouder, 2 ounces of cloves grossly beaten, one ounce of Nuttmegg, one ounce of Cinamon all grossely beaten, halfe a pound of Liquorish as much Anniseeds. Steep all these close covered 24 houres and then distill it in an Alembisk with a soft fire, but you must remember to put a bread shilling in the bottom of the pott to

keep it from burning. This water is good for the
yellow jaundies, and likewise for a surfeit taking 2 or
3 spoonfulls in a morning and fast for an hour after,
and it will cause an appetite and a sweet breath, and
it will repell everything from the heart.

Aqua Cælestis

Take a Gallon of Gascogne wine, Ginger, Gallingall,
Cinamon, Cloves, Nuttmegg, Mace, Anniseed of each
an ounce, Sage, Mint, Red Rose, time, Camomile,
Lavender, of each a handful. Beate the spices small
and bruise the herbs. Putt them all in the wine, and
let them stand 12 hours stirring it diverse times then
still it in a Lembick, and keep the firste pint by itself,
it is the best thing to comfort the spirits, preserve
youth and is a helpe against all diseases that come of
Cold, it is good against the shaking palsy, cures the
Contraction of the sinnews, kills wormes in Children.
It is good for cold in the gutts, comforts the stomack,
cures the cold dropsy, helps the stone in the bladder,
it is good to preserve health by taking a spoonfull in
4 or 8 days.

A wound drink good for all manner of ulcers or imposthumes or inward bleeding or to disgest or carry any thing off the stomack

Take 20 ounces of crabs eyes prepared, put it into a
stone bottle that holds a gallon. Put to it 2 quarts of
the best old white wine. Corke it, and tye it down

very hard and close. Set it into a Kettle of boyling water, and put hay round about it, lay a stone on the top of it to keep it down to the bottom of the kettle, let it boyle well 2 houres and set it down gently till it is cold, for if you open it before, it will all flye out of the bottle. Drink a sack glass of it in the morning, and at 4 a clock in the afternoon or at anytime if the stomack be out of order, you may when this quantity is used put two quarts or more of wine to the same poured ordering it as at first, only let it boyle full 2 hours. Keep it allways in the same bottle and pour it out gently.

An approved Experiment on severall barren Weomen Especially on the Dutches of Gulisk, who after an unfruitful marriage of 20 years became a Joyfull Mother of many Children

Take Wall Rue, the Inner bark of Juniper wood, fumitory, veratram, wth there roots and agrimony the roots of each a handfull, yellow jaundies 2 ounces, sweet marjoram, ffennell, Lavendar and Camomile of each one handfull, shredd all those things, and put them into a bagg, boyle it into a sufficient quantity of water for a bath, let the patient sit in it for the part of an houre, let the water reach a little above the navell, it being of a moderat heate, and so supplyed to that degree of heat during bathing time, beginning 4 dayes after the time of her monthly elimanations forbearing all manner of fruits dureing that time.

Plague Water

Take Sage, Sellondine, Rosemary, Rue, Wormwood, Mugwort, peny royal, Dragon, Scabious, Agrimony, Balme, Spodium, Comfary, Carduns, Betony, Rosasols of each one handfull, Angelico roots, henbane roots, Tormentall roots, zadory roots, liquorish of each half an ounce, slice the roots and wash the herbs, and dry them well in a cloath, shredd them and put them alltogether in a gallon of white wine. Let them steep 2 days and 2 nights close covered, put them into a cold still and drain it off softly, keep the water in pinte bottles and sweeten it with Sugar Candy half an ounce for a bottle, the first running will be worth 8.8 a quarter.

Stomack Lozenges

Take Cinamon, Cloves and Nutmegg of each 2d worth and a little Ginger. Make them all into pouder and foarth them, then take half a Gill of Rosewater and as much faire water and one pound of loafe sugar, boyle your sirup till you believe it Candy, then put in your pouder, stirr them well together, then drop or rather poure them on your papers, being first strewed with frothed sugar.

Against Loosnes

Make a Caudle of a pound of rise as you make one of oatmeale, and give it Lukewarme with a little grated

Cinamon and what sugar you please, give Likewise diverse times Marmalad of Quinces in your Spoon.

A Cordiall water

Still Isquebagh over again in a Cold Still with Rose Solis, Angelico, a little Rue, Sparemint, and a little wormewood drawn off with care, and tended with wett cloaths.

A Cordiall water to sweeten the blood or an Almond milk for the purpose

Take some strawberry leaves, 2 handfulls, one of violet Leaves, Savory and Maidenhaire a handfull clean pickt, and washt, and infused in 6 quarts of water, take currans a pound cleare washt and bruisd and close covered till a quart or three pints be dissolved, and when cold strain and wring it hard and beat of Jordan Almonds 6 ounces, and after blanched with some of the liquor keep them from boyling still as you beate them, strain them and put the liquor you strain into the other and it will be Almond milke and first and last at 4 in the afternoon drinke half.

Poppy Water

Take 4 pecks of poppyes. Bruise them and put them into a Gallon of Brandy to steep severall dayes, and after you have strained them out to the liquor 4 ounces of white Anniseeds & 2 ounces of Corriander Seeds, one ounce of Cardamom. Let all the Seedes Compounded. One pound of Raisons of the Sun stonded, one pound of figgs sliced, halfe an ounce of Liquorish sliced, and if you like Spearemint or Angelico you may put halfe a handfull of each to it, after they are steept 14 days, strain it and sweeten it with sugar to your taste.

Or you may make the syrup of poppyes and bottle it up and the other ingrediants above mentioned may be put in the Brandy as above and so make it into a water & at your pleasure may put as much of the syrup as may make a poppy water in the same manner as you put syrup of Clove Gillyflower in Brandy.

To make spirit water

Take 4 quarts of Aquevitch not of the strongest, and 2 pound of white sugar Candy, a pinte of poppies also poppie water, a pinte of Bourage water, a pound of figs, a pound of Raisons of the Sun stoned and the figs are to be sliced, 2 good handfulls of Red Rose buds, slipping off the whites, a little handfull of Rosemary as much of Red Minte, as much of sweet Marjoram, and as much of unsett Hysop and 40 Cloves, put all those together in a glass with the Aquavitch and let them stand in the sun or else in some hott place by the fire. The best time to make it is in june, becaus all the herbs must be green you must steep it marvelous close.

For the Ricketts

Take maiden hysop, maidenhaire and Coltsfoot of each quarter of a handfull, Anniseeds, Coriander seeds, of each quarter of an ounce, Liqourish halfe an ounce, 2 ounces of Raisons of the Sun stoned, 2 figgs sliced. Boyle all those together in 3 pintes of Spring water till half be consumed, strain it and put to the Cloves 2 ounces of brown sugar candy, bruise the seeds and Liquourish, let the child drink often of it.

An oyntment for the same

Take Rosemary, Bay leaves, Camomile, Lavendar tops, Maiden hysop, Maiden Time of each one handful. Allhoof, Comfry, of each halfe a handful. Shred the herbs and pound them in a mortar, and boyle them in a pound of butter out of the Churn an houre. Strain it out and annoynt the Childs sides and knees, and down to his feet, overstroaking up his hips evening and morning for quarter of an houre, this is best to be made in May. Let the child bleed in the ear when the sign is below the heart. Roll and swing the child, if they be livergrown and bound in their bellyes give them syrup of Damask Roses, and flower of white Brimstone, mingle it all together, and lett the Child eate thereof on the point of a knife two or three times a day.

To Cure a Consumption

Take a Calves Liver, and a litle of the
Lungs, and Cutt them in thinn slyces,
and put them togethor, then take a good
handfull of sage and cutt it through, and
still them togethor, and drinke the water
3 or 4 times a day, this hath Cured a Consum=
=ption and herhirk father when furr gone

Another

Take a good handfull of Ground Ivie
and pound it with 3 or 4 spoonfulls
of ale, then straine it and let the party
Drinke it 4 mornings 3 spoonfulls at
a time, and drinke Broth or whitewine
afterwards which they please, it must be
Drunke 21 dayes, takeing it 3 mornings
and Leaving it 3 mornings

So

To Cure a Consumption

Take a Calves Liver, and a litle of the Lungs, and cutt them in thinn slyces, and put them together, then take a good handfull of sage, and cutt it through, and still them together, and drinke the water 3 or 4 times a day, this hath Cured a Consumption and [cho]lick feaver when far gone.

Another

Take a good handfull of Ground Rice and pound it with 3 or 4 spoonfulls of Ale, then strain it and let the party drink it 4 mornings 3 spoonfulls at a time, and drink Brew or white wine afterwards which they please, it might be drunk 21 days, taking it 3 mornings and Leaving it 3 mornings.

For the Wormes

Take of wormeseed 4 ounces, senna one ounce, Coriander seed prepared, harts horne of each half a dram Rubarb halfe an ounce, dryed Rue 2 drams, beate them into pouder, of this pouder give to a young child as much as will stand upon a groat, to those of ryper years as much as will stand upon six pence, to a man or woman as much as will stand on a shilling, it must be given in honey, they must fast for an houre after, and then take posset drink.

A Plaster for the Wormes

Take of Lemon foarthe 4 penyworth, oxitropium 2 pennyworth, oxgall as much as will moisten it to be neither too soft nor hard, 5 cloves of Garlick cutt small and put upon a peece of Lambs leather from Navel to Stomach.

A Syrup for the Scurvey

Take 3 partes of Sea Scurvy Grass and one parte of watercress. Pick them and wash them very clean, bruise them, and strain the juyce into a silver bason if you have it and set it over a clear fire, and when it is ready to boyle, strain in the juice of a good Lemon. It will raise a green thick Curd and so run it through a strainer, and when it is cleare, put in as much fine sugar as will make it a syrup, not too thick, when it is cold bottle it up, and put 3 spoonfulls in a draught of warme ale every morning or evening. This syrup hath wrought many great and strange cures, and is a most sovereign remedy for the scurvey, and so is syrup of Elderberryes.

Poppy surfeit water

Take 2 Gallons of Brandy & put therein as many poppy leaves as the brandy will cover and let them steep therein 3 days then take out halfe the poppies & put therein a handfull of sparemint, a handfull of Balme, a handfull of Marygold flowers, Burrage flowers, CloveGilly Flowers of each one handfull, and one handfull of Cardus. Let these steep for a weeke and then strain them all out, & put thereto halfe a pound of Raisons stond, halfe a pound of figgs sliced, halfe a dozen of Dates, half an ounce of Anniseeds, an ounce of Coriander seeds bruised, halfe an ounce of Liquorish sliced, a quarter of an ounce of Mace, halfe quarter of an ounce of Cloves, 3 or 4 Nuttmeggs pounded let these steep 3 weeks, and then strain all out and sweeten and bottle up for your use.

For Convulsion fitts

When the party is going into a fitt, give to a child, a good spoonfull of the juice of Betony, made thick with whole sugar Candy. If it be a man or a woman you may give 2 or 3 spoonfulls as you see occasion. This taken for 9 mornings cures the head ach.

A Water against Miscarriage

Take the white of 21 eggs beaten very well, and put to them 3 pintes of new milk and still these in a cold stille, stirring it often for feare of burning, and after 3 days drink a wine glass every morning and at 4 o'clock in the afternoon, sweeteneth with white sugar candy. To prevent miscarriage drink a draught of cold spring water the first and last thing you do night & morning.

A soveraign water devised by Dr Stephens wch the Archbſp of Canterbury Useing did may cures with it, the D^r kept it as a secret till he was on his death bed and then gave it to the Bſp as followeth

Take Ginger, Gallingall, Cinamon and as many cloves, Anniseeds, fennell seeds, Carway seeds, of each a quarter of an ounce, then take sage, mint, Red Roses, Tyme, Pollitory, Rosemary, Wilde Tyme, Cammomile, Lavendar of each a handful. Breake your Spices finely and bruse your herbs small, put them into a Gallon of white or red wine, and let them stand so infused the space of 12 hours often times stirring them and then still them all in a limbeck over a soft fire, keep the first water by itself for its best the second is good but not so good add a handfull of marygold flowers, a handfull of wormwood, a handfull of Curds and Rue. This water prospereth health, can ease long life and is a good remedy against many diseases. It is much better it stand all summer in the sun. It is good against the shaking palsy, it cureth the contracting of the sinnews, it helpeth conception in women that are barren, it killeth wormes in the belly, It cureth an old cough, helpeth the toothach, cureth the Dropsy, It helpeth the stone and the reyns of the bard, It cureth a stinking breath and maketh one look young.

Another of Dr Stephens waters

Take a Gallon of good wine, Galligall, Ginger, Cinamon, Nuttmegg, Cloves, Anniseed, Carraway seeds of each a dram, sage and mint, Red Roses, wild tyme, Allicampane roots, pollitory of the red rosemary,

Camomile of each a handful, the spices being finely beaten and the herbs washed and small pounded. Put altogether in the wine standing all night Covered and so distill them.

This water Comforts the heart and spirits and helps all manner of defects and many of cold. It helps women to concieve that have long been without Children, it killeth wormes in the belly, it cureth an old cough, it easeth the toothach, it comforts the stomach very much, it maketh the dropsy, it helpeth the stone in the bladder, Rheynes and back in violent coughing. Give a spoonfull of syrup of Diadocum, with conforte of roses and Olibanum.

A Cordiall Water

Take two handfulls of Dragons, of wormwood, Angelicoe, Balme, Mint and Cardins of each two handfulls, still all those in a cold still with a quart of sack.

Another Cordiall Water

Take 2 quarts of sack and put it to a good handfull of Rosemary as many tops with the blossoms, as much cowslip flowers, as much Betony, as much sweet marjoram, Angelicoe, Dragon and Balme and as much marigold flowers. Putt Nuttmeggs, Cloves, Cinnamon and Mace half an ounce of each, one ounce of harts horne, let them lye two or three days and nights in the sack, stirring them up every day, then poure them into a Rose still with 2 ounces of mitherdate, of Friar's 6 pennyworth of saffron. Lifte up your still, and let it drop upon white sugar candy, when you take it put sugar in it.

Plague Water

Take sage, Sellondine, Rosemary, Rew, wormwood, Mugworts, Pennyroyall, Dragon, Scabious, Agrimony, sorghum, comfrey, cardin, cowslip, Betony, Rosasols of each a good handfull, Anyslix roots, herbane roots, Tomentill roots, zedary roots, and liqourish half an ounce of each. Slice the roots and wash the herbs, shake them and dry them in a Cloath, shred them and put them altogether into a Gallon of white wine, then let them stand two nights and two days in steep those covered, put them into an oldmary still. Draw off your water into pinte and quart bottles, your smallest serve Children, give 4 or 5 spoonfulls of it warme at a time and to an older body you may give more.

Dr Burgess Prescription against the Plague

Take 3 pieces of Muscadin and boyle it with a handfull of sage and as much Rue till one pinte be wasted then strain it and sett it over the fire again, and put therein one pennyworth of Long pepper, half an ounce of ginger, a quarter of Nuttmegg, all beaten together, let it boyle a little then put thereto 4 pennyworth of Mitherdate, 2 pennyworth of Triakle and a quarter of a pinte of Angelicoe water, take thereof constantly, or for prevention take half a spoonfull or if already infected take 2 or 3 spoonfulls, halfe the morning and halfe the evening, sweating upon this is good against the distemper or other infectious diseases, as the small pox, measles, and feavers. Zadary is good to chew in your mouth in case of infection.

Bβp of Killmore for the Scurvy
I know no better remedy for the scurvy than to take a quart of the juice of it, and put it into a square glass bottle and squeez the juice of an orange into it, and strain it, let it stand till it be cleare and drink 3 or 4 ounces fasting and as much in the afternoon, and continue this course for 2 months and it will not grow cleare in a round bottle.

Dr Whartons dyet drinke
for the Scurvy and Dropsy
Take Colts foot, Scabious, Mallows, spotted Lung-wort of each 3 handfulls, raisons of the sun stoned a pound, 6 dates, 15 cubebs, Harteshorne, Ivory and prunes of each an ounce, Anniseeds, sweet fennell seeds of each halfe an ounce, sea Scurvy grass a handful, Liquorish an ounce, bran halfe a handful, 2 Nuttmeggs bruised, 5 Gallons of Ale, a pound of Damsons seedes bruised, Burdock root 4 ounces. All these things must be hanged in a bagg in the Ale.

For the Toothach

Joy of the wall boyled in white wine vinegar and Constantly held in the mouth take away all pain.

Mother Ashby's Purge

Take one ounce of syrup of Buckthorne and halfe an ounce of syrup of Rubarb in a little warme possett drink, take heed that you take no Cold and it will work directly and very safely.

A very good glister against winde and may be taken in a fitt of the stone or Collick

Take wormwood, ffever few and Cammomile of each a small handfull, a good spoonfull of Cumin seeds, a piece of fatt mutton. Boyle all together in 3 pintes of faire water till halfe be consumed then strain it, and put into the Liquor 4 spoonfulls of brown sugar and as much sallott oyle and so give half of it at a time, or a whole pint it will give 4 or 5 stools.

Another Glister for the winde

Take mallow Leaves, the herb Marjory, groundsell, Camomile the flowers thereof, ffeaverfew, still tyme, of each a handful. Boyle them in a quart of faire water till one half is boyled away. Strain it and in 3 quartes of a wine pint of the liquor mingle 4 handfulls of Coarse sugar, the yolk of one egg, 2 spoonfulls of

Sallott oyle or a piece of butter and a little salt, this makes your glister to draw down the winde.

ꙮ

To stopp bleeding
Take a nettle root washed and scraped & chew it in your mouth. It seldom fails.

ꙮ

Madam March for a Stitch
Take a draught of midle ale warmed and strew in a spoonfull or two of good oatmeale to drinke.

ꙮ

A good oyle for the worm
Take a good handfull of savon, the like of Rue, the like of wormwood, the like of feaverfew, the like of Lavendar cotton, the like of uncutt leeks, shred all these together, then take a quart of sack and a quart of sallott oyle and put altogether into a brass pott or bottle, boyle altogether upon a little fire until such time as you cannot distinguish the sack from the oyle. Keep and annoynt therwith the stomach and the navel.

ꙮ

To Cure the Country disease if it turn to a flux
Take one pound of new butter out of the Churn and melt it, take it the heat of a glister in a glister bagg.

For a Cough

Take a pipkin containing a gallon, fill it full of spring water, and put into it 10 leaves of Hartshorne, a reasonable handfull of Liverwort, an ounce of Maidenhare, of covash, Coltsfoot, Anniseed of each an ounce, a like quantity Allicampane roots, 30 raisins of the sun stoned and finely sliced thinn, all which sett over a fire untill it be halfe boyled away, then let it sett and till it be cold, then strain it, and put to it 2 pounds of double refined sugar, and let it Coole and strain it again. You may use it as you have occasion, taking 3 spoonfulls as you go to bed and so in the morning.

For a Wheezing & Stopping

Take the fine powder of Allicampane one spoonful, of honey 2 spoonfulls and of sugar 2 spoonfulls. Mingle these together and take as much as a small wallnutt every morning and evening.

໒ᥱ✦ᥤ໑

An Approved Medicin for Consumption

Distill the pimpernell that beareth the red flower, still it when it is in blossom, take of the water 3 or 4 spoonfulls and 6 or 8 spoonfulls of milk warme from the Cow, and a little fine sugar, or whole sugar candy. Mingle these together and let the party drink it as warme as they can get it from the cow for 2 or 3 weekes together in the morning and two hours before supper, if in the morning they may sleep after it, then leave taking it for a fortnight, then take it again.

To Ease the Stone and Loose the belly
Take Elder Berrys when they are ripe, dry them in a shade or cool oven, and pound them to pouder, and take as much of it as will lye upon a six pence, in a draught of warm ale morning and evening first and Last.

For the Stone
Take a spoonful of the syrup of Althea, as much oyle of sweet almonds newly drawn, a spoonfull of honey with 2 yolks of eggs, newly laid, but beate them all well together with some nuttmegg sliced. Put into possett drinke made of white wine and ale, stir it well and drink warm and walk upon it.

For the Wormes
Take Consett Leeks, mother of tyme, rue, wormwood of each a handfull, shred them and boyle them in white wine vinegar, till the herbs be tender, then put them up in a bagg, and lay them between the navell and stomack, keep the vinegar to warm it, and apply it 3 nights together.

An Excellent Comforter of the Stomack and a helper of Digestion
Take 2 ounces of good Conserve of roses, of chosen mother water 2 drams, mingle them together, and

when you are going to bed, eate thereof the quantity of a hazill nutt. This will repell all flatulence or windings of the stomach, it drives away vain humors and venemous vapors, the good digestion dryeth the rhume and strengtheneth the sight and memory.

A Remedy for the Dropsy hott or Cold

Take of the tops of Archangel or blind nettle, and red sage of each a small quantity. Stamp them together and strain the juice of them into some Ale that is stale, so much as will serve to drink morning and evening and (Godwilling) it will afford the cure.

Another for the Dropsy wch hath cured many a person when they were left and forsaken by the phisicians

Take greene broome and burne it in some cleane place that you may save the ashes of it, take 10 or 12 spoonfulls of the same ashes, and boyle them in a pinte of white wine till the virtue be in the wine, then coole it and drain the wine from the dreggs and make 3 draughts of the wine, only fasting in the morning, the other at 3 in the afternoon and the other when you go to bed, this seldome failes in its desired effect.

An Excellent Dyet Drink for the Spring
to purge the blood and Cleanse it

Take halfe a peck of scurvy grass of Brooklime, water cress, Agramony, maidenhaire, liverworte, Burrage, Bugless Buttony, Sage, Sweet Marjoram, some wormwood, hypps of green hops, fumitory of each a good handfull of Ivory, Hartshorne and yellow jaundies of each an ounce, parsely flower, Asparagus, roots of each an ounce, raisins half a pound. Boyle those very well in a gallon of beere working together.

The Bean Cod water for dissolving the Stone

Take a peck of green Beancods without dew or rain and 2 good handfulls of Saxifrage and another of Beancods and so distill in this manner a quart of water and then distill another quantity from the green beanpod alone, and drink of both of there waters, if the patient be most troubled with the rheins then let him take most frequently of the plain bean water but upon the coming down of things gravall or stone let him drink of the other.

To Prevent an aching tooth to Cure it
or make a hollow tooth Drop out of it selfe

Every morne wash your mouth with white wine in which sperryye hath been boyled, and you shall never be troubled with the toothach. If your tooth be hollow & paineth your mouth take this herb called Spinnage and squeez it and mingle wheat flower wth it. With that make a pill or paste, and fill that cavity of your tooth therewith, Leave it there a while chewing it every 2 houres and the tooth will fall out.

*D*ʳ *Dun's bitter drinke*

Senna halfe an ounce, Cardin seeds halfe, tips of Comfrey and of Cammomile flowers almost halfe a handfull, Gentian roots and scimples, infuse all this in a pinte of Spring Water and give it to the child to drinke at morning.

For a Cold or Consumptive Cough

Take halfe a pounde of Raisons of the Sun, stalk & stone them, wᵗʰ 4 ounces of sugar candy beate them to a paste, & when they are well beaten, add to them halfe a pound of good old Conserve of roses 30 drops of the spirit of vitriol then beate them all very well together, and so keep it covered in a pott very close, for your use, then take of this paste or Conserve about the quantity of a large nuttmegg in the morning, fasting at 3 a clock in the afternoon and at bed time.

For the Scurvey

Take Scurvy Grass, water grass, brook tyme, Dandolyn and sage of each a like quantity. Cutt them small, pound them in a wooden mortar, squeez the juice out and with a Clean Cloath sett them on a skillett over a soft fire till it boyle, then put in the white of an Egg to clarifie it. Take it off, and when it is coole put it in a bottle with the peel of a civil orange. About 6 o'clock in the morning take 2 spoonfulls of it in any liquor, with about 24 drops of the spirit of hartshorne, and so walke upon it eating nothing for 2 or 3 hourse, after dinner you may take the like quantity for 2 or 3 times.

For the Chollick
Take 3 or 4 Cloves of Garlick and bruise the Garlick in a poringer and let the Garlick so bruised stick to the bottom of the poringer, and put the mouth of the poringer over the navil, and within a quarter or halfe an houre, it will dry away the pain. This is an experienced remedy by severall persons who to my knowledge have been cured when all other things have failed.

For a Consumption or decay of the Lungs
If you take tobacco kindle your pipe with Brimston marsh, do this severall times that you make suck in the smoak of the Brimston and if your lungs be washed inparte it will make sound and perforce what parte of the lungs are Left though crumpled[?].

For the Goute

Take a little of the Glovers Leather whilst the Allum
is in it, and upon the said Leather putt a plaster made
of black soap mixed with the yolk of an Egg separated
from the white. Lay it on the Leather being pricked
wth the point of a knife or Bodkin, and apply to the
place grieved. If it go from thence to any other joynt
or place follow it with the like plaster and it will drive
the Goute quite away, this hath been experienced wth
good success.

To Cure the Ricketts or weakness of the Limbs & Back

Take two Coal black hens dress them as if they were
for the Spitt, gather about a quarter or 3 pintes of
black snailes, or as many as will stuff the bodys of
both hens with the snailes, put in a fire, with the
bigness of an egg of sweet or May Butter, and baste
the hens very well, the snailes will drop & conform to
a small thing in the bodyes of the hens, the Oyle that
drops from the hens keep for use to annoynt the
Child with.

Another

Take 2 black sheeps head and a handful of Rue and a
handful of Lavendar, boyle altogether to a Jelly &
skim off the fatt. Bath the child wth the broath and
anoint wth the fatt.

For a Dropsy

Take 5 or 6 Grains of Resin, of Syrup of Buckthorn, of Resin of Salop more less according to the Constitution and 24 grains of Cream of Tartar, strew being well mingled in halfe a pinte of warme ale to drink it up. Keep yr selfe warme.

For a Flux & will also help gripings in the Gutts

Take a quart of new milk, the bigness of a Wallnutt of Comfort of Roses as much cinnamon beaten to powder as will heap upon a shilling, boyle the milk wth those ingredients till it come to a pinte, then take it off. This is a very good remedy and with the yolks of 2 eggs beaten and some sugar cure it between 2 cups or tankards as you do butter ale till all is incorporate. Drink it off going to bed, of it bring a breathing sweat. It will do well, but you need not force a sweat, this is a good cure in twice or thrice using of it, if your stomack be so weak that you cannot take ale at night you may take in the morning what you can't at night.

An Excellent oyntment good for severall Cures

Take foxglove, Agrimony, Balme, Germander, Lavender spike, Bay Roots, Liverwort, Ground Rew, Marsh, bane, Cellondine, Chickenweed, Quick Grass, Brook tyme, Ducksmeate, Sugared Mader, Alexander, Spleenwort, Rosemary, Wild Tansy, Verbine, Adders Tongue, Butterbur, Couslips of each a large handfull pickt clean, cutt small, beaten a little in a mortar. Take a sufficient quantity of May Butter with one quart of Neats Foot oyle put all into an earthen pott stopt up close. Put the pott under ground for the space of one & twenty days with horse dung round the pott and under the bottom of it, and when you take it up boyle all over an easy fire close stopt for the space of 4 or 5 houres, strain all the Liqour out, there is severall things to be added to it, if you will go the cost of it.

For a Consumptive Cough

Rare and excellent had from the Earl of M... who depend on it. Take of Allicampane, unsett Hysop, Coltsfoot, Rough Barley of each a handfull, Hoarhound halfe a handfull, Liquourish 2 ounces, Anniseeds one ounce, 4 or 5 cloves of Garlick. Boyle these in 6 quarts of Spring water till it consumes to near a quart, then strain it, and add a pound of sugar, and boyle it to a syrup take a spoonfull thereof in the morning and another at night.

For Gravell or Stone

Take Cammomyle well pounded & take the juice about a spoonfull in warme ale or white wine, and so drink it.

Spring water with a spoonfull of honey and drink in the morning fasting is good.

An Excellent Cordiall

Take the Root Gallingall, Zodery Calameus Aromaticus, Gentian, Long pepper, Bayberrys of each one dram cloves, of each half a dram, of Cinamon one spoonfull, Angelica Root one dram, all those bruised, and putt into a Bottle of Brandy of 3 pints and let them stand 3 days before the fire, then take a spoonfull of it after being strained in half a pynt of warm ale for use as warm as you can drink it, this for a man or woman or half a spoonfull for a child at any time.

Mrs Skeen's Cordial

Take of Roots call'd Gentian, Ganangall, zedoarie Calamus Aromaticus, Bay Berries, long pepper, Lignum Nephrittium of each one dram, aloes, Cinnomon, Angelicoe roots. Accrus of each a dram, let them be grossly bruis'd and infuse 'em in a quart of right Nant's brandy. Cork it close & put a piece of Hon'd leather over it. Cover & set it to ye fire burning, stew for three days & shake it very often. Then after this is straind put in more Brandy to ye Ingrediants left of ye other & this will make a weaker sort of cordial. The way to know when the right done is to try it in a silver spoon which if it wil be clamy, and look yellow as saffron. This cures and prevents all consumptions, Imposthumance, Cholick & gravel to admiration.

An aproved Medson for a tickling or Consumtive Cough: this is Mukleroys Medson

Take a pint of hony, 3 ounces of Sugar Candy, 1 ounce of powder of Alicompaine, pound the sugar Candy very fine & mix it with the Alicompaine & hony in a mug, it will hold above a quart. You may sharpen it with a little white wine vinegar then cover it with paist and put it in the oven with rouls.

Mrs Wentworths poultis for Any Old Sore or Venomous Swelling

Take wheat flower & boyle it with Milke the thickness of a poultis. Boyle a litle honey in it. When you take it off the fire put in a spoon full of Sallad oyl or any other oyl you think proper. When it is cold enough to use put in a litle barm.

Mrs Brays Reciepts

To make A Green Ointment

Lavendar Flowers, White Lillies, Red Roses, of each two handfuls. half a pound of hoggs lard, 3 pints of the best sweet Sallott oyle, one pound and ½ of Mutton Suett, one pound & ½ of Deer Suett, one qʷᵗ of cream, one pound of fresh butter, put the cream with ye oyle & other ingrediants together & boyle them two or three times in a week. First time let them boyle well but afterwards just simmer and keep them stirring constantly a quarter of an hour til they are very hot, then take them of the fire & keep them very close in the pot you boyle them in for a month or five or six weeks until you think all the virtue is out of the herbs, then strain it out into Galley potts & leather over the paper, which the vertue may be preserved & not decay.

❧

To make A Sear Cloath for a bruise, pain or hurt in the back or elsewhere

Take half a pound of black pitch and half a pint of oyle, a quarter of a pound of red lead beaten to a pouder, put your pitch & Oyle together, the pitch melted first with the oyle (be careful it does not run over) & when 'tis melted, put in your red lead & stir it about, if you think its too hard, put in a little hogs lard & then put it into a bason of waer & rowl it up into a salve & spread it upon Leather for y^r use.

❧

To make A green Salve for A Cut any raw Sore or green Wound

Take half a pound of Bees Wax clear & good, half a pound of white resin, one ounce of Venice Turpentine, a quarter of a pint of sweet oyle (if not to be gotten about the bigness of an Egg of Hoggs Lard) about the quantity of a nutmegg of Verdygrease (beat to powder) put them altogether (except the verdigrease which must be put in last) in a new Earthen pott or Pipkin, & when they are all in & melted take them off the fire & keep them stirring & when done put it into a bason of water, & make it up into a Roll for use.

To make an infallible Water for a Sore Mouth & Eyes, it will cure an Ulcer, Canker, Scurvey or any Sore breeding in the Mouth or Throat (it's call'd Old Dogg) & is likewise good to wash & apply where a Dogg has bitt

Take half an ounce of white camphire, one ounce of white Copperas, one ounce of Bole Almanack, a piece of Beach Allom, about the biggness of a nuttmegg, you must take of Allom, Copperas, & Camphire & beat them in a Pestle & Mortar. Mince the Camphire very small (but don't burn them altogether in a fireshovel with the other ingredients) you must boyle 3 pintes of water & when the water boyles (take of your Copperas, Camphire, & Allom & beat them very small, & then put in the Bole Almanack, & pound them together) put them all in together into the boyling water & when you think it had boyled away about a pint take it off the fire & when its cold, shake it, & put it into a Bottle & as you use it draw it off the fire into a vial, always let it settle in the vial before you wash y^r mouth.

For the Eyes

Take half a pint of the Old Dogg above prescribed drawn off clear in a vial & put in one penny worth of Tutty (pounded very fine) & one spoonfull of Honey

& when you use it shake it keep your head back &
your eye lids open & the vial close to your eye lids
use it at night when you go to bed & shake it (& if
your eyes are very bad) in the morning before you
rise.

14

Cosmetics, Skin, and Hair Care

To make Pomatum

Take the kidneys of veale hott and putt them in spring water and hanging them twice a day for 9 days, if the weather be hott not so long beate it well with the end of a Rolling pin and take out all the strings, then put it into a close quart pott or flagon, when stopped close put it into a pott of seething water and let it boyle 3 or 4 hours then take it off and strayn it them sett it over a slow fire again skim and cloase it but let it not boyle too much, but just rise, then strain it out upon a wett plate or into a little pott.

Another for Pomatum

Take a Hoggs Caule hott out of the belly and put it into Springe water. Change it twice a day for 9 days together,then take it out, beate it very well taking out all the strings, then weigh half a pound and to that 2 ounces of white Lilly roots and 2 ounce of pippins and so add an ounce of double refined sugar finely sifted through tiffony & put it into a Close pott putt into frothing water and let it boyle until the apple and root be soft, then take it off strain it and keep it for your use.

Wash it in rose water till it be white then take a wett Cloath and wring it and spread it on a clean board or table and with a spoon drop them here or there in little Cakes, paper them up and keep them, but never make too many of them at a time for they will not keep, you may put spermaceti in any of these, or wash them with orange flower water or make it with lambe if you please.

An Excellent Pomatum

Take one shillings worth of white Lilly roots, cutt off the yellow, string them, wash them clean and brake them take the like quantity of Marsh Mallows scrape off all the back skin and peel them from the pith, then take 12 pound of the caules of mutton, putt from the sirop and put them into Conduit water, and when they are cold peel off the skin and take out all the skins and Kernels then put it into fresh water for 9 days hanging it twice a day, then put it into new milk for a day and a night, then dry it with a clean sheet and with a stick brake it till it be dry like powder, then put the roots and sewett together into an earthen pott with a narrow mouth stopt close, and sett it into a kettle of water over a great fire, till it be melted, then strain it into an earthen pan and let it stand til it be cold, then keep it for store.

Take a quarter of a pound at a time, putt it into a Gally pott and melt it into a skillet of water and scrape

it into an earthen pott that holds a pottle, and stirr it,
beate it all one way for two hours or it will Curdyle
and Spoyl the best time to make it is either in the
Spring or Fall, and it will keep for a whole year.

(❧)

A Water for the haire

Take southernwood, Dill, and Ribworts of each a
handfull, Dillseeds & Nuttmegg of each an ounce,
then putt them into a Gallon, mingle them well and
distill them, when you use the water take 2 drops of
the oyle of southernwood and Dill and mix with it
then wett your haire with it.

(❧)

A Pouder for the haire

Take the roots of Cypress 4 ounces, Callamus
arromaticcus 4 ounces, Bean flower half a pound,
Benjamin 2 ounces, Red Rose leaves 4 ounces,
Liquor Aloes one ounce and a halfe, Muske and Civit
of each 10 Grams and Red Corall and white Amber of
each an ounce, mix them all and beate them to fine
powder.

(❧)

A Most Excellent oyle for the face

Take Almonds Blanched 3 ounces, oyle of white
Mastischt 3 ounces, whites of new laid eggs 4 ounces,
Camphrey an ounce, Gumdragon 2 ounces. Beate all
these very well and let it rest 6 days, save that you

must beate and stir it once a day, then beate it in a pan, and putt it in a lemon bagg to strain out the oyle in a press and therewith anoynt the face or skin.

It makes the skin smooth, cleare and white, it preserves youth, keeps the face from wrinkles, kills any inflammation, takes away all spotts and freckles. It is the best that ever was found out for this purpose, you may make a soap cloath out of it that is good for most things.

⟨❦⟩

A water for the face

Take the whites of 40 eggs, Allom an ounce, one pynt of best Rosewater, beat them thouroughly together, then stille in in a Cold still and morning and evening wash your face with this water.

⟨❦⟩

Or this for heate in the face

Every morning drink a glass of old Mulligan sack, and eat a little toast dipped in it.

If you find much heat in it you would have to purge. You may know by your hand if it be hott or dry or if you find an inward heate.

⟨❦⟩

A Paste for the hands

Take two pound of bitter Almonds blanched and beaten, then take two ounces of the Cold seeds, an ounce of poppy seeds, an ounce of naturall Balsome, an ounce of bacon, 12 grains of Camphor, the yolks of two new Eggs, a stale white penny loafe and pinte and a halfe of new milke. First take the crums of bread and put them into a little milke, and mix them, take the Almonds and mix them, put them into an earthen pipkin where you boyle them then take your Eggs and mix them with some milke, then put in your Cold seeds, still adding a little milke and the poppy, Borax, Camphor and Balsome, mix it by little and little thus the quantity of milke be spent then set it over a soft fire till you find it curdle, with a soft curd in the bottom, if it burns it is spoyled.

15
Household Tips

To clean Silver Lace

Take the lace of from your garment and lay it upon a table and with a brick rub it all over Very well with bruised Allum beaten fine till you find it become of the right Colour then shake it very well with a Clean lining cloth Oftentimes over.

Guide to Weights
and Measures

This book was written before weights and measures were standardized as today. Even now, although the US and the UK use the same terms for weights and measures, the actual amounts described by those words are slightly different, as they were standardized separately. These weights and measures are therefore intended to give a general indication rather than a precise guide to quantities!

Dram: either of two units of weight: (1) an avoirdupois unit equal to 27.343 grains (2) an apothecaries' unit equal to 60 grains. There are three scruples in a dram.

Gallon: a unit of liquid capacity equal to 231 cubic inches. There are eight pints in a gallon.

Gill: a British unit equal to ¼ imperial pint or 8.669 cubic inches.

Grain (graine): a unit of weight based on the weight of a grain of wheat taken as an average of the weight of grains from the middle of the ear.

Ounce: any of various units of weight based on the ancient Roman unit equal to $\frac{1}{12}$ Roman pound. There are eight drams in an ounce.

Peck: either of two units of dry capacity equal to $\frac{1}{4}$ bushel.

Pint (pynt): any of various units of capacity equal to $\frac{1}{2}$ quart. There are sixteen fluid ounces in a pint.

Pottle: Two quarts (or a container that holds that amount).

Quart: any of various units of capacity, that is, a British liquid or dry unit equal to $\frac{1}{4}$ imperial gallon or 69.355 cubic inches.

Scruple: unit of weight equal to 20 grains, used by apothecaries.

Winchester measure: an old English series of measures originally made standard at Winchester, England.

Glossary of Words and Ingredients

The plants and herbs in the Glossary (with their scientific names in *italics*) are all native, relics of ancient cultivation or cultivated in gardens in Ireland and Britain unless otherwise described (e.g. the exotic spices). Many of them are also known to have been used in traditional folk cures. It was not possible to identify all the ingredients in the recipes and cures with certainty, so in some cases plant names are suggested. Obvious ingredients, such as parsley and nutmeg, are not included in the Glossary.

Adders Tongue: A wild fern, Adder's-tongue (*Ophioglossum vulgatum*).

Agramony, Agrimony: Agrimony (*Agrimonia eupatoria*) or Fragrant Agrimony (*Agrimonia procera*), wild plants.

Ague: A fever or shivering fit similar to the symptoms of malaria.

Alembisk, Allembisk: The Alembic, a distilling appara- tus, now obsolete, consisting of a rounded, necked flask and a cap with a long beak for condensing and convey- ing the products to a receiver.

Alexander: Alexanders (*Smyrnium olusatrum*), a relic of an- cient cultivation; used as a pot-herb, also in mead and metheglin.

Alhoof, Allhoof: Ale-hoof; another name for wild

Ground-ivy (*Glechoma hederacea*).

Allicampane, Alicompaine: Elecampane (*Inula helenium*), an ancient herb; bitter aromatic roots were used in herbal medicine.

Aliments: Food; nourishment.

Alloe, Alloes, Aloes: Aloe (*Aloe*), succulent plants, some with medicinal properties.

Allom, Allomm, Allum: Potash, an alkaline potassium compound, especially potassium carbonate or hydroxide.

Althea (Syrup of): Marshmallow (*Althaea officinalis*); used as both a medicinal and ornamental plant.

Amber, Ambergreece, Amber greese, Ambergreese: Ambergris, a wax-like substance that originates as a secretion in the intestines of the sperm whale, found floating in tropical (and other) seas.

Angelica, Angelico, Angellico, Angelicoe: Angelica, a tall aromatic plant of the Parsley family, with large leaves and yellowish-green flowers. It is used in cooking and herbal medicine and was introduced into Europe from Syria in the fifteenth century.

Anyslix: Possibly a reference to anis, *Anisum*.

Aquavitch, Aquevitch: Aquavit. Defined by the Oxford English Dictionary as an alcoholic spirit made from potatoes or other starchy plants, from Akvavit in Norwegian, Danish and Swedish. However, the OED gives a nineteenth century origin for this word in English, suggesting that this is a much earlier example.

Archangel: Probably White Dead-nettle (*Lamium album*) or Yellow Archangel (*Lamiastrum galeobdolon*), both in the Mint family.

Balsome: Balsam, an aromatic resinous substance, such as balm, exuded by various trees and shrubs and used as a base for certain fragrances and medical preparations.

Bandle Cloath: Linen.

Bane: One of a number of plants thought to be poisonous.

Barberry, Barrberry: A shrub, wild Barberry (*Berberis vulgaris*) or a garden Barberry (*Berberis*); produces berries.

Barm, Barme: Yeast or leaven.

Bartholomew Tide: The evening before the feast day of St Bartholomew.

Bayberry: Fruit of the Bay tree.

Bean flower: Bean flour.

Benjamin: A spelling by popular etymology for gum benzoin, the resin of various trees of the genus Styrax.

Betony: Probably the wild plant Betony (*Stachys officinalis*), but the common name can refer to other species.

Black jaundies: Black jaundice: Weil's disease, a bacterial infection of the liver.

Blind nettle: Perhaps White Dead-nettle (*Lamium album*); not related to the stinging Nettle.

Bodkin: A thick, blunt needle with a large eye, used for drawing tape or cord through a hem.

Bole Almanack: Bole-Armonick or Armenick. Various types of friable soil were known as bole. That which came from Armenia (hence "armonick") contained clayey earth and was used for diarrhoea.

Bolus: A thick substance rolled into a ball, esp. for medical use.

Borage, Bourage, Burrage: Borage (*Borago officinalis*), a garden plant.

Borax: A white compound which occurs as a mineral in some alkaline salt deposits and is used in making glass and ceramics, as a metallurgical flux, and as an antiseptic.

Brawn, Brawne: Meat from a pig's or calf's head that is cooked and pressed in a pot with jelly.

Brimston, Brimstone, Brimston Marsh: Sulphur.

Brooke Tyme: Probably Brooklime (*Veronica beccabunga*), found by streams and in other wet places.

Broom, Broome: Wild shrub, Broom (*Cytisus scoparius*) or perhaps a garden Broom.

Buckthorne: A wild shrub, Buckthorn (*Rhamnus catharstica*); known for its purgative properties.

Bugless: Perhaps Bugloss (*Anchusa arvensis*).

Burberrys: See Barberry.

Burdock: Any of several closely related species of wild *Arctium*.

Burgumys: Bergamot, a type of citrus fruit.

Buttela: Battalia, a pie of titbits such as sweetbreads and cockscombs.

Butterbur: *Petasites hybridus*, a wild plant.

Buttony: See Betony.

Callamus arromaticcus: Sweet-flag (*Acorus calamus*); calamus, a preparation from the aromatic "root".

Camphor, Camphire, Camphrey: Camphor. A white volatile crystalline substance with an aromatic smell and bitter taste, occurring in certain essential oils.

Candy height: Point in boiling at which sugar starts to candy, or change substance.

Candying pott: Saucepan suitable for preparing sugary substances such as syrups, jams, etc.

Canker: A painful sore, generally in the mouth.

Carbonade: Carbonnade, to cook on hot coals.

Cardin, Cardon, Cardun, Carduus: A kind of Thistle.

Carway: Seeds of Caraway (*Carum carvi*).

Castle soap: Castile soap, soap made of olive oil.

Cataplasm, Cataplasme, Cattaplasm: Plaster or poultice.

Caudle: A drink or sauce of wine or beer, thickened with other substances.

Caule: Caul, Omentum.

Cellondine: Celandine, either garden Greater Celandine (*Chelidonium majus*) or wild Lesser Celandine (*Ranunculus ficaria*), two unrelated plants.

Chaffing dish: Chafing dish, a metal pan containing burning charcoal, used for cooking at table.

Chaldron: The entrails of an animal.

Chickenweed: Probably Chickweed (*Stellaria media*); the name "Chickenweed" was also used for Groundsel (*Senecio vulgaris*), both common weeds in cultivated ground.

Chobles: Unknown. Perhaps the plural of a dialect word meaning 'to eat, to scrunch'.

Civet, Civit, Civot, Civott: A strong musky perfume obtained from the secretions of the civet's scent glands.

Civil orange: Seville orange.

Clary: Probably a garden Sage (*Salvia*).

Clovegilly, Clove gillyflower, Clovegillyflower, Clovegillyflower Jack: Carnation pink.

Codlins: Codlings. Any of several varieties of cooking apple having a long tapering shape.

Coffins: Pastry (occasionally paper or clay) cases.

Cold seeds: The seeds of various cucurbitaceous fruits (as the melon or cucumber) sometimes used as emollients.

Collop: A slice of meat.

Colts Foot: Colt's-foot (*Tussi-lago farfara*), a wild plant.

Comfary, Comfrey, Comfry: Wild or garden Comfrey (*Symphytum*).

Conduit water: Fresh water that has not been standing still.

Confits, Confort, Conforte: Comfit. A sweet consisting of a nut, seed, or other centre coated in sugar.

Confusion: Consistency.

Consett leeks: Possibly leeks associated with Consett, a town in Co. Durham, England.

Copperas: Green crystals of hydrated ferrous sulphate.

Corall: Coral.

Corans: Currants.

Corne poppys: Probably the weed of corn fields, Corn Poppy (*Papaver rhoeas*), or a closely related red-flowered Poppy.

Courb: Possibly a reference to curving or bending the meat in the pie, as opposed to cutting it into pieces ("courb" being an obsolete verb meaning to cure or bend).

Couslip: Cowslip (*Primula veris*), a wild plant.

Covash: Perhaps cohosh (*Cimicifuga racemosa*).

Cubebs: Tropical shrub (*Piper cubeba*) in the Pepper family, producing pungent berries and related to Black Pepper.

Damask Roses: A common type of Rose.

Diadocum: Diadochite, a mineral consisting of a basic hydrous ferric phosphate and sulphate that is brown or yellowish in colour.

Discuss: Disperse, get rid of.

Distemper, Distempers, Distempters: A viral disease causing coughing and fever.

Dragon, dragons: Perhaps Tarragon (*Artemisia dracunculus*).

Dropsy, Dropsyes: Oedema, abnormal accumulation of fluid beneath the skin or in the body's cavities.

Ducksmeate: Duckweed (*Lemna*, probably *Lemna minor*), an aquatic plant.

Duretick: Diuretic.

Electuary: A medicinal substance mixed with honey or another sweet substance.

Elimanations: Natural loss of fluids from the body; "monthly elimanations" are menstruation.

Eyebright: Probably a species of wild *Euphrasia*; traditionally used as a remedy for eye problems; "Eyebright" is also used for an unrelated Speedwell (*Veronica chamaedrys*).

Faggott: A little bundle (of herbs, in this case) tied together.

Feaver few, Feaverfew, Ffeaverfew, ffever few: Feverfew (*Tanacetum parthenium*), a garden plant; used in herbal medicine to treat headaches and other ailments.

Ffleabame: Fleabane (*Pulicaria dysenterica*), a wild plant; reputed to drive away fleas.

Fflower: Flour.

Ffluxe, Flux: Flux. The discharge of fluid substances from the body, such as diarrhoea.

Fforce, Force, Forse: To push through a sieve or mincing device, to mince, e.g. forced balls are balls of mincemeat, meatballs.

Ffrankinsence: Frankincense, an aromatic gum resin obtained from an African tree and burnt as incense. Also called "olibanum".

Fitts of the mother: Hysteria or a feeling of choking, thought to be caused by the womb rising in a woman's body.

Flagon: Large container in which drink is served, typically with a handle and spout.

Flixweed: *Descurainia sophia*, formerly a medicinal herb; thought to cure dysentery.

Foarced: Forced.

Foarth, Foarthed: Forced.

Friars: Presumably Friar's Balsam, a solution of benzoin resin in alcohol.

Friccasee, Friccasie: Fricassee.

Frume, Frumeing: Refers to the scum or foam that often forms on a boiling substance.

Fumitory: One of several species of Fumitory (*Fumaria*), common weeds.

Gally pott, Galley pott: Gallipot, a small pot made from glazed earthenware or metal, used by pharmacists to hold medicines or ointments.

Galligall, Gallingal, Gallingall, Ganangall: Galangal, an Asian plant of the ginger family, the aromatic rhizome of which is widely used in cookery and herbal medicine.

Garbush: To remove the innards, from "garbage", or the internal parts of an animal.

Gentian: Perhaps a garden Gentian; this name was also applied to gentian-like wild plants, e.g. Field Gentian (*Gentianella campestris*) and Common Centaury (*Centaurium erythraea*).

Germander: Perhaps wild Germander Speedwell (*Veronica chamaedrys*).

Glister: Clyster. A medicinal enema.

Glovers leather: Soft leather of a suitable quality for making gloves.

Gras pepper, Grass paper, Grass pepper: Cress, a garden plant.

Gravel, Gravell: In medicine, kidney stones.

Groat: A coin.

Ground Rew: See Rue.

Groundsell: Groundsel (*Senecio vulgaris*), a weedy plant.

Gumdragon: A name for Tragacanth, a natural, water-soluble gum obtained from the dried sap of several species of Middle Eastern legumes.

Hartechock, Hartichock: Artichoke.

Harts horne, hartshorn, Hartshorne, Harteshorne: Hartshorn, an aqueous ammonia solution used as smelling salts, formerly prepared from the horns of deer.

Hawthorne bottoms: Hawthorn (*Crataegus monogyna*); buds and young leaves are edible.

Hempseeds: Seeds of Hemp (*Cannabis sativa*).

Henbane: *Hyoscyamus niger*, a poisonous plant.

Hens grease: Chicken fat.

Herons: Herrings.

Hoarhound: Black Horehound (*Ballota nigra*) or White Horehound (*Marrubium vulgare*), both in the Mint family with a tradition of use in medicine, especially for coughs and colds.

Holdloafe: Container or tray to use when baking bread.

Honsleek: Evidently Honeysuckle.

Hupe: Hoop.

Hysop: Hyssop (*Hyssopus officinalis*), an aromatic plant used in cookery and herbal medicine.

Imposthume, Impostumance: A collection of pus or purulent matter in any part of the body; an abscess.

Isquebagh: *Uisce beatha*, the Irish word for whiskey.

Ivory: Presumably vegetable ivory, a plant substance found in a number of trees, in the form of a nut in the case of the ivory palm, and used as a substitute for ivory, or maybe shavings of actual ivory.

Japp Green: A food colourant.

Jaundies: Jaundice.

Jordan almonds: A high-quality almond of a variety

grown chiefly in southeastern Spain.

Joy of the wall: Possibly the vernacular name for *Galium murale* (where Galium has been misundersood as Gaudium).

Lapis Callaminarus, Lapis Callamintus: Calamine.

Laudanum: Tincture of opium.

Lights: The lungs of animals such as sheep or cattle, for food.

Lignum Nephrittium: A traditional diuretic derived from the wood of two tree species, Mexican Kidneywood and Narra.

Liquor aloes: A liquid preparation of Aloes (see above).

Limbeck: Alembic, an apparatus used in distillation.

Livergrown: Having breathing difficulties, or being swollen in the stomach area. Possibly from *Lebertran*, a dialectal German folk term for cod-liver oil.

Liverwort, Liverworte: A group of primitive non-flowering plants, or an unidentified herb used for liver problems.

Lobb: Lobe.

Long Pepper: Any of several species of Pepper (*Piper*).

Lye: A strong alkaline solution, often obtained by leaching ashes.

Mackroons: Macaroons.

Mader: More likely wild Woodruff (*Galium odoratum*) than the related cultivated Madder (*Rubia tinctorum*), the latter grown for its dye.

Magott: Magpie.

Maiden hysop: A variant of Hysop (see above).

Maiden time: Perhaps a variant of the herb Thyme.

Maidenhaire, Maiden haire, Maidenhare, Maidonhaire: Maidenhair, any of several unrelated plants including the common fern Maidenhair Spleenwort (*Asplenium trichomanes*).

Makerall: Mackerel.

Manshott, Mannshott, Mainshott: Manchet, a loaf of the finest kind of wheaten bread.

Mallows: See Marsh Mallows.

Marrow: Bone marrow, presumably bovine.

Marsh: Presumably *Meirse*, a feminine noun in Scottish Gaelic meaning *Apium graveolens* "wild celery".

Marsh Mallows: Marsh Mallow (*Althaea officinalis*), grown and used as both a medicinal and ornamental plant.

Mastik, Mastischt: Gum mastic, Mastiha, a chewy product made from the sap of Lentisk trees.

May Butter: Butter made in the month of May.

Maullolet: Apparently a cooking technique.

Mellilot:, Mellilott: One of several species of Melilot (*Melilotus*).

Mirch: Chilli pepper.

Mitherdate: Mithridate, an antidote for poison.

Mojoaram: Wild or garden Marjoram (*Origanum*).

Morphen: Morphea, localised scleroderma.

Mother water. Also "mother liquor", a residual liquid resulting from crystallisation that remains after the substances that readily or regularly crystallize have been removed.

Mugwort: *Artemisia vulgaris*, known for a long time as a medicinal herb.

Muscadin: Perhaps "Muscadine". A group of species and varieties of grape native to Mexico and the south-eastern US.

Musk, Muske: Musk, a strong-smelling substance secreted by the male musk deer.

Neats foot oyle: An oil made from the feet of cattle.

Neats tongues: Bovine tongues.

Nitre: Saltpetre.

Oldmary still: Evidently, a particular type of still for the distillation of alcohol.

Olibanum: Frankincense.

Oringade: Orangeade.

Oxgall: Bile secreted in a bovine gall bladder.

Oxitropium: Probably related to Oxytropis, a genus of plants of the legume family.

Pallott: Palate.

Palsy: Paralysis often accompanied by a feeling of numbness.

Papp: Soft, solid matter; mush.

Penny Royall, Pennyroyall, Peny Royal: Pennyroyal (*Mentha pulegium*), a mint-like plant used in herbal medicine.

Pilt: Peeled.

Pimpernell: Scarlet Pimpernel (*Anagallis arvensis*), a wild plant.

Pipkin: A small earthenware pot or pan.

Pippins: Red and yellow dessert apples.

Pitch: A sticky, resinous black or dark brown substance that is semi-liquid when hot and hardens when cold, obtained by distilling tar or turpentine.

Pizzle: Penis.

Plasine: Unknown.

Plumes: Plums.

Plurisie: Pleurisy, a disease of the lungs characterised by painful respiration.

Pollipodium: Any of three closely related wild Polypody ferns (*Polypodium*).

Pollitory: Perhaps Pellitory-of-the-wall (*Parietaria judaica*).

Pomander: Aromatic substances enclosed in a perforated bag or box and carried as a guard against infection.

Pomatum: Pomade.

Porphory: Porphyry, a hard igneous rock containing crystals of feldspar in a fine-grained groundmass.

Porringer, Poringer: Porringer, a small bowl, typically with a handle, used for soup, stew, or similar dishes.

Possett, Posset: Posset, a drink made of hot milk curdled with ale, wine, or other alcohol, and typically flavoured with spices.

Postalls: Pastilles, aromatic or medicated lozenges.

Potage: Thick soup.

Probatum: Proof of efficacy.

Puffball: A fungus that produces a spherical or pear-shaped fruiting body which ruptures when ripe to release a cloud of spores.

Pullatt, Pullott: Pullet, a young hen.

Quartans: A mild form of malaria.

Quibibs: Perhaps an alternate spelling of "Cubeb" (see above).

Quick Grass. Probably Common Couch or Scutch-grass (*Elymus repens*).

Quick lime: A white caustic alkaline substance consisting of calcium oxide, which is obtained by heating limestone and which combines with water, with the production of much heat.

Rank: Foul or foul-smelling.

Red lead: A red form of lead oxide used as a pigment.

Rennet, Rennutt, Rennitt: Curdled milk from the stomach of an unweaned calf, containing rennin and used in curdling milk for cheese.

Rezin of Galop: This may be resin of julep, a confection of mint and sugar.

Rheins, Rheyns, Reyns: Kidneys.

Rhume: Rheum, the emission of liquid mucus.

Ribworts: Probably wild Ribwort Plantain (*Plantago lanceolata*); also used to stop bleeding.

Ricketts, Rickitts: Rickets, softening of the bones as a result of a deficiency in Vitamin D.

Ringo roots: Roots of wild Sea-holly (*Eryngium maritimum*) or a garden *Eryngium*.

Rosasols, Rose Solis: A species of Sundew (*Drosera*), a carniverous plant which grows in bogs.

Rosin: Resin, especially the solid amber residue obtained after the distillation of crude turpentine oleoresin, or of naphtha extract from pine stumps.

Roules: Bread rolls. Presumably, "cream of" refers to crumbs made of the inner part.

Rue: Cultivated aromatic Rue (*Ruta graveolens*), used in herbal medicine.

Rynes: Kidneys.

Sack: A dry white wine formerly imported into Britain and Ireland from Spain and the Canaries.

Sallott oyle: Oil suitable for dressing a salad.

Saltpeter, salt peter, Saltpetre: Potassium nitrate.

Salve: An ointment.

Samphire: Rock Samphire (*Crithmum maritimum*), a coastal plant; its fleshy leaves can be eaten and pickled.

Sarsnett: Sarsenet, a fine, soft silk fabric, used as a lining material and in dressmaking.

Sassafrass, Sassafass. A North American tree, Sassafras (*Sassafras albidum*), with aromatic leaves and bark; leaves can be infused to make tea or ground.

Savon: Perhaps savin (*Juniperus*).

Savory: One of a number of herbs of this name.

Saxifrage: Wild or garden Saxifrage (*Saxifraga*).

Scabious: Wild Devil's-bit Scabious (*Succisa pratensis*), related Field Scabious (*Knautia arvensis*) or a garden Scabious.

Scimples: Simples, a generic term for medicinal plants.

Scurvy, Scurvey: Scurvy, a disease resulting from a lack of Vitamin C.

Scurvy Grass, Sea Scurvy Grass: One of several Scurvygrasses (*Cochlearia*), coastal plants rich in vitamin C; formerly eaten, especially by sailors, to prevent scurvy.

Scutcheonele: Scutchanele, to colour with cochineal.

Sellondine: Celandine; either cultivated Greater Celandine (*Chelidonium majus*) or wild Lesser Celandine (*Ranunculus ficaria*), two unrelated plants.

Senna: The dried pods of the Senna tree.

Sewett: Suet.

Shaking palsy: Paralysis with involuntary tremors.

Shelot: Shallot, a type of onion.

Sillibub: Syllabub, a sweet dish based on cream.

Sippets, Sippetts, Sipits: Small pieces of bread or toast, used to dip into soup or sauce, or as a garnish.

Slack, Slake: To combine quicklime with water to produce calcium hydroxide.

Skirrets: An East Asian plant of the Parsley family, formerly cultivated in Europe for its edible carrot-like root.

Small beer: Weak beer.

Smelt: Food dye.

Sorghum: A cereal which is native to many tropical and sub-tropical areas.

Southernwood: An aromatic shrub (*Artemisia arbrotanum*).

Sparemint, Spearemint: Spearmint (*Mentha spicata*), a garden plant.

Sparrowgrass: Asparagus.

Spermaceti: A white waxy substance produced by the sperm whale, formerly used in candles and ointments.

Sperryye: Possibly Meadowsweet (*Filipendula ulmaria*), which contains salicylate; formerly called *Spiraea filipendula*.

Spike: Presumably a valerianaceous plant, probably *Valeriana officinalis*.

Spleenwort: Probably the common wild fern, Maidenhair Spleenwort (*Asplenium trichomanes*).

Spodium: Burned bone, used for medicinal purposes, or a type of ash, often made by burning stone pyrites or from smelting zinc or copper.

Spotted Lungwort: Lungwort (*Pulmonaria officinalis*), a garden plant with spotted leaves.

St James Tide: The evening before the feast of St James.

Succory: Also known as Chicory (*Cichorium intybus*); cultivated; young shoots blanched for use as salad.

Suiett: Suet.

Surfeit: An illness caused or regarded as being caused by excessive eating or drinking.

Tansy: 1) *Tanacetum vulgare*, with aromatic leaves, formerly used in cookery and medicine. **Wild Tansy** could refer to Silverweed (*Potentilla anserina*). 2) A type of dessert.

Taplash: The dregs of ale or liquor.

Tertian, Tertians: A form of malaria causing a fever that recurs every second day.

Tiffony: Tiffany, thin gauze muslin.

Tomentill, Tormentall: Tormentil (*Potentilla erecta*), a wild plant with roots rich in tannin.

Tutty: A yellow or brown amorphous substance that is obtained from the flues of furnaces smelting zinc and that consists of a crude zinc oxide.

Umbles: The innards of an animal.

Venise Treacle: A medical "electuary" of various herbs and spices in a honey emulsion, for treating poisoning and so called because Venice was the main centre of production for a long time.

Veratram. Perhaps garden False-helleborine (*Veratrum*), a poisonous plant.

Verbine: Probably Vervain (*Verbena officinalis*), or perhaps a garden *Verbena*.

Verdygrease: Verdigris, a bright bluish-green encrusta-tion or patina formed on copper or brass by atmospheric oxidation, consisting of basic copper carbonate.

Verjuice, Verjuis: A sour juice obtained from crab apples, unripe grapes, or other fruit, used in cooking and formerly in medicine.

Vermillion: A brilliant red pigment made from mercury sulphide.

Vertiginous: In this context, presumably dizziness.

Vitriol, Vitrioll: Either copper sulphate or ferrous sulphate.

Wall Rue: Probably the common wild fern Wall-rue (*Asplenium ruta-muraria*).

Wardens: A type of pear.

Water grass: Water-cress (*Nasturtium officinale*).

Water trefoil: Bogbean or Buckbean (*Menyanthes trifoliata*), found in bogs.

Whitloe, Whitlow: Whitlow, an abscess in the soft tissue near a fingernail or toenail.

Woodcock, wood cock: A woodland bird of the Sandpiper family, with a long bill, brown camouflaged plumage, and a distinctive display flight.

Wormeseed: Wormseed (*Artemisia cina*).

Wormwood, wormewood: *Artemisia absinthium*, with aromatic leaves, used medicinally and as an ingredient of vermouth and absinthe.

Worte: Wort, the sweet infusion of ground malt or other grain before fermentation, used to produce beer and distilled malt liquors.

Yce: To ice or glaze.

Yellow jaundies: Perhaps Ragwort (*Senecio jacobaea*).

Zadary, Zadory, Zedary, Zedoarie, Zeodory, Zodery: An Indian plant related to Turmeric, with an aromatic rhizome.

Zimper: Simmer.